MathFlare

Name: ________________________

Class: __________

Teacher: ________________________

Introduction

As parents and educators, we recognize the pivotal role mathematics plays in shaping a child's academic journey and future success. Yet, the path to mathematical proficiency can often seem daunting, fraught with challenges and complexities. That's where the transformative power of MathFlare Workbooks shine through, illuminating the way forward with clarity, precision, and purpose.

Introducing MathFlare Workbooks – a beacon of guidance, a testament to excellence, and a catalyst for achievement. Crafted with meticulous care and expertise, MathFlare Workbooks stand as paragons of educational excellence, designed to nurture young minds, ignite a passion for learning, and develop a deep-rooted understanding of mathematical concepts.

Picture this: your child eagerly delves into the pages of Mathflare Workbook, greeted by a step-by-step guide illuminated with vivid examples that demystify complex mathematical concepts. With each turn of the page, they embark on a journey of discovery, encountering thoughtfully curated practice questions that reinforce learning and hone problem-solving skills. And when they unveil the answers to those very questions, a sense of accomplishment blossoms within them – a tangible reward for their hard work and dedication.

But MathFlare Workbooks are more than just tools for learning; they are pathways to comprehension, fostering a deep-seated understanding of mathematical concepts through a sequential, logical flow. From fundamental principles to advanced problem-solving strategies, every chapter builds upon the last, ensuring a robust foundation upon which future knowledge can be constructed.

As parents, we yearn for nothing more than to see our children thrive, to witness the spark of inspiration ignited within them as they conquer academic challenges with confidence and poise. MathFlare Workbooks serve as partners in this noble endeavor, offering not just practice questions, but the keys to unlocking a world of opportunity.

And for teachers, MathFlare Workbooks stand as invaluable allies in the quest to cultivate mathematical proficiency in the classroom. With answers readily available, instructors can focus on guiding and nurturing their students, confident in the knowledge that MathFlare Workbooks provide a solid framework upon which to build.

In the pages of MathFlare Workbooks, we find not just the promise of academic excellence, but the seeds of a brighter tomorrow. So let us embrace the power of mathematics, let us champion the journey of learning, and let us pave the way for a generation of young minds poised to shape the world. With MathFlare Workbooks as our guide, the possibilities are infinite, and the future, bright.

Table of Contents

MathFlare
MATH WORKBOOK
Grade 2
Step by Step Guide and Essential Practice with Answers
Addition Subtraction
Multiplication
Place Value and Expanded Notations
Geometry
MathFlare Publishing

MathFlare
MATH WORKBOOK
Grade 2-3
Step by Step Guide and Essential Practice with Answers
Addition Subtraction
Multiplication and Division
Place Value and Expanded Notations
Geometry
MathFlare Publishing

MathFlare
MATH WORKBOOK
Grade 3
Step by Step Guide and Essential Practice with Answers
Multiplication and Division
Decimals
Place Value and Expanded Notations
Fractions and Geometry
MathFlare Publishing

MathFlare
MATH WORKBOOK
Grade 1
Step by Step Guide and Essential Practice with Answers
Counting and Numbers
Addition and Subtraction
Place Value and Expanded Notations
Understanding Time
MathFlare Publishing

MathFlare
MATH WORKBOOK
Grade 1-2
Step by Step Guide and Essential Practice with Answers
Counting and Numbers
Addition and Subtraction
Place Value and Expanded Notations
Understanding Time
MathFlare Publishing

MathFlare
MATH WORKBOOK
Grade 3-4
Step by Step Guide and Essential Practice with Answers
Addition Subtraction
Multiplication Division
Place Value and Expanded Notations
Fractions and Geometry
MathFlare Publishing

MathFlare
MATH WORKBOOK
Grade 4
Step by Step Guide and Essential Practice with Answers
Addition Subtraction
Multiplication Division
Place Value and Expanded Notations
Fractions and Geometry
MathFlare Publishing

MathFlare
MATH WORKBOOK
Grade 4-5
Step by Step Guide and Essential Practice with Answers
Multiplication Division
Place Value and Expanded Notations
Fractions and Geometry
Unit Conversion
MathFlare Publishing

MathFlare
MATH WORKBOOK
Grade 5
Step by Step Guide and Essential Practice with Answers
Multiplication Division
Place Value and Expanded Notations
Fractions and Geometry
Unit Conversion
MathFlare Publishing

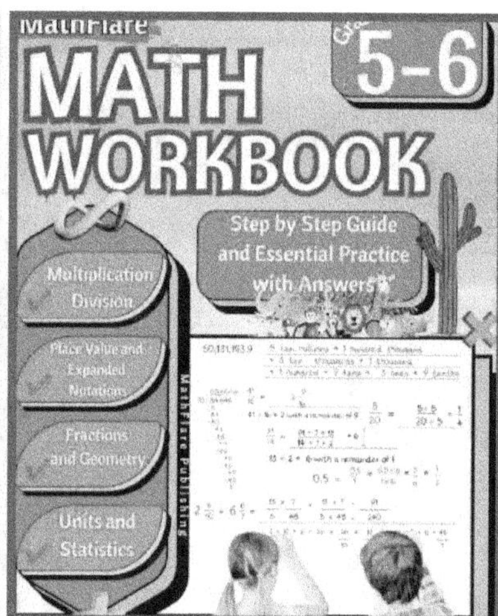

MathFlare
MATH WORKBOOK
Grade 5-6
Step by Step Guide and Essential Practice with Answers
Multiplication Division
Place Value and Expanded Notations
Fractions and Geometry
Units and Statistics
MathFlare Publishing

MathFlare
MATH WORKBOOK
Grade 6
Step by Step Guide and Essential Practice with Answers
Integers and Statistics
Arithmetic and Pre-Algebra
Fractions and Geometry
Ratio and Percentage
MathFlare Publishing

MathFlare
MATH WORKBOOK
Grade 6-7
Step by Step Guide and Essential Practice with Answers
Arithmetic and Pre-Algebra
Ratio, Percent Proportion
Geometry
Statistics
MathFlare Publishing

MathFlare
MATH WORKBOOK
Grade 7
Step by Step Guide and Essential Practice with Answers
Pre-Algebra
Ratio, Percent Proportion
Geometry
Statistics
MathFlare Publishing

MathFlare
MATH WORKBOOK
Grade 7-8
Step by Step Guide and Essential Practice with Answers
Pre-Algebra
Ratio, Percent Proportion
Geometry and Cartesian Plane
Statistics
MathFlare Publishing

MathFlare
MATH WORKBOOK
Grade 8-9
Step by Step Guide and Essential Practice with Answers
Pre-Algebra
Ratio, Proportion and Percentage
Linear Equations
Geometry and Cartesian Plane
MathFlare Publishing

MathFlare
MATH WORKBOOK
Grade 8
Step by Step Guide and Essential Practice with Answers
Pre-Algebra
Percentage
Linear Equations
Geometry
MathFlare Publishing

Addition and Subtraction

Addition with Regrouping

When we do addition, we combine numbers. But sometimes, when we're adding
numbers, we might need to regroup. Regrouping means we have to move a number
from one place to another, usually to the next column, to get the right answer.

For Example: Let's take an example of adding 6533 and 7579 together:

$$5\ 6\ 5\ 3\ 3$$
$$+6\ 7\ 5\ 7\ 9$$

First, we start by adding the digits in the ones place: 3 + 9 = 12. We write down
the 2 in the ones place and carry over the 1 to the tens place.

$$1$$
$$5\ 6\ 5\ 3\ 3$$
$$+6\ 7\ 5\ 7\ 9$$
$$2$$

Now, we add the digits in the tens place, along with the carry-over: 3 + 7 + 1 = 11.
We write down the 1 in the tens place and carry over the 1 to the hundreds
place.

$$1\ 1$$
$$5\ 6\ 5\ 3\ 3$$
$$+6\ 7\ 5\ 7\ 9$$
$$1\ 2$$

Now, we add the digits in the hundreds place, along with the carry-over: 5 + 5 + 1 = 11. We write down the 1 in the tens place and carry over the 1 to the hundreds place.

$$
\begin{array}{r}
1\ 1 \\
5\ 6\ 5\ 3\ 3 \\
+\ 6\ 7\ 5\ 7\ 9 \\
\hline
1\ 1\ 2
\end{array}
$$

Now, we add the digits in the thousandth place, along with the carry-over: 6 + 7 + 1 = 14.

$$
\begin{array}{r}
1\ 1\ 1 \\
5\ 6\ 5\ 3\ 3 \\
+\ 6\ 7\ 5\ 7\ 9 \\
\hline
4\ 1\ 1\ 2
\end{array}
$$

Now, we add the digits in the ten-thousandth place, along with the carry-over: 5 + 6 + 1 = 12.

$$
\begin{array}{r}
1\ 1\ 1\ 1 \\
5\ 6\ 5\ 3\ 3 \\
+\ 6\ 7\ 5\ 7\ 9 \\
\hline
1\ 2\ 4\ 1\ 1\ 2
\end{array}
$$

This process of carrying over helps us accurately add numbers, especially when they're larger.

Subtraction with Regrouping

Subtraction is a key math operation where we find the difference between two numbers. Sometimes, when we subtract, we might need to regroup, which means borrowing from the next column.

Let's take an example of subtracting 8436 from 6563:

First, we start by subtracting the digits in the ones place: 3 - 6.

Since 3 is less than 6, we need to regroup. We borrow 1 from the tens place, making it 5 tens instead of 6, and add it to the ones place.

So, 3 becomes 13, and then we subtract 6.

$$8 \quad 5 \quad 6 \quad 13$$
$$-6 \quad 4 \quad 3 \quad 6$$
$$7$$

Now, we subtract the tens place digits: 5 - 3 = 2

$$5$$
$$8 \quad 5 \quad 6 \quad 13$$
$$-6 \quad 4 \quad 3 \quad 6$$
$$2 \quad 7$$

Now, we subtract the hundreds place digits: 5 - 4 = 1

$$5$$
$$8 \quad 5 \quad 6 \quad 13$$
$$-6 \quad 4 \quad 3 \quad 6$$
$$1 \quad 2 \quad 7$$

Now, we subtract the hundreds place digits: 8 - 6 = 2

$$5$$
$$8 \quad 5 \quad 6 \quad 13$$
$$-6 \quad 4 \quad 3 \quad 6$$
$$2 \quad 1 \quad 2 \quad 7$$

This process of regrouping or borrowing helps us accurately subtract numbers, especially when the top digit is smaller than the bottom one.

Let's solve problems from exercises:

$$\begin{array}{r} \overset{\scriptstyle 1\ 1\ \ 1\ 1}{59{,}574} \\ +\quad 6{,}576 \\ \hline 66{,}150 \end{array} \qquad \begin{array}{r} 97{,}120 \\ -\quad 7{,}383 \\ \hline 89{,}737 \end{array}$$

Addition (3 Addends)

To add three numbers (3 addends) together, we simply add them one by one.
Let's solve a problem.

$$\begin{array}{r} \overset{\scriptstyle 1\ 1\ 1}{6{,}533} \\ 4{,}727 \\ +\quad 6{,}102 \\ \hline 17{,}362 \end{array}$$

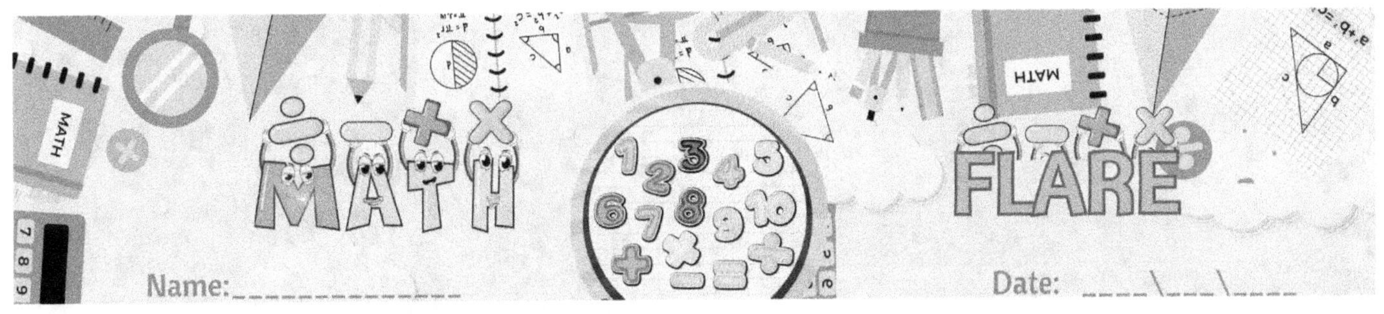

Addition with Regrouping

Find the sum.

1. 23,456 + 8,675	2. 47,917 + 3,999	3. 72,835 + 9,789	4. 67,458 + 4,974
5. 52,171 + 8,949	6. 93,717 + 9,496	7. 52,161 + 8,979	8. 25,649 + 6,878
9. 11,598 + 9,663	10. 77,866 + 4,256	11. 61,918 + 9,396	12. 11,668 + 9,568
13. 57,647 + 6,693	14. 58,643 + 4,589	15. 29,381 + 7,939	16. 89,683 + 3,947
17. 38,345 + 7,979	18. 71,135 + 9,987	19. 87,582 + 8,829	20. 36,413 + 4,997

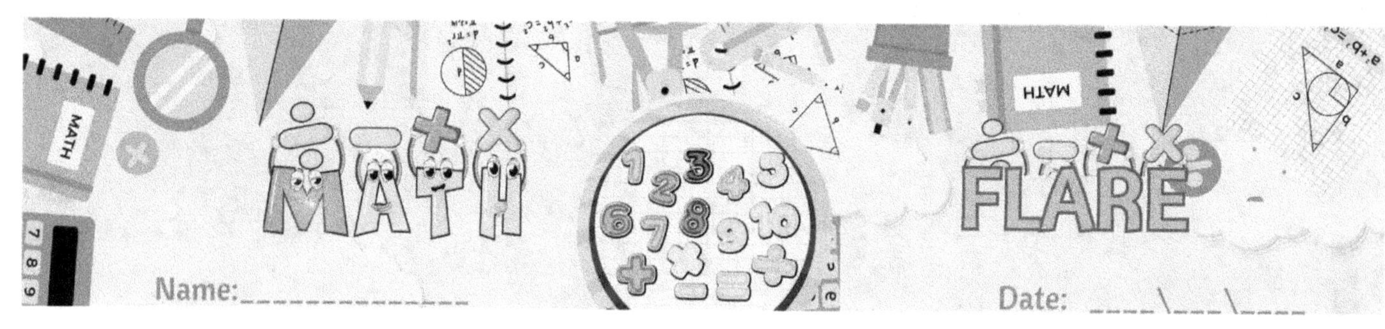

21. 11,648 + 9,598	22. 62,627 + 8,784	23. 91,185 + 9,975	24. 63,811 + 9,499
25. 79,512 + 2,998	26. 96,975 + 8,736	27. 41,158 + 9,983	28. 23,185 + 8,998
29. 24,679 + 6,751	30. 61,747 + 9,683	31. 28,876 + 3,436	32. 99,759 + 7,362
33. 33,729 + 9,498	34. 65,722 + 8,698	35. 95,983 + 9,537	36. 74,211 + 8,999
37. 44,216 + 9,894	38. 41,559 + 9,582	39. 71,837 + 9,487	40. 89,216 + 6,995

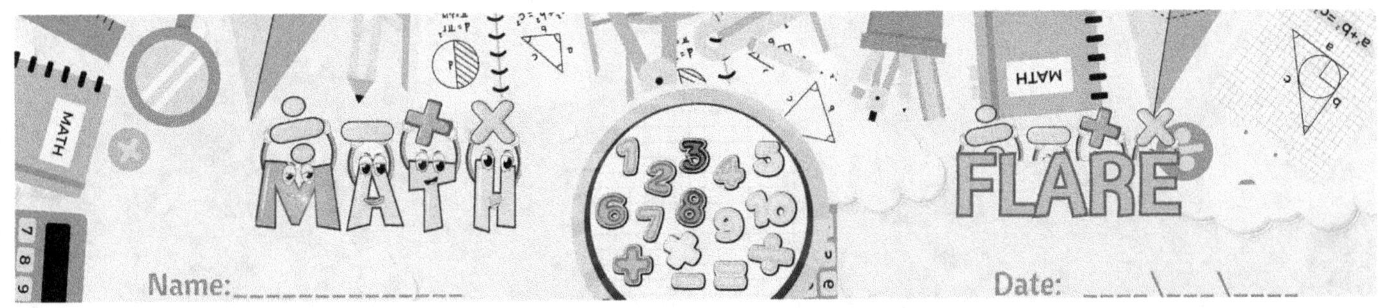

41. 96,631 + 6,989	42. 63,611 + 7,499	43. 82,171 + 8,959	44. 98,958 + 8,797
45. 57,913 + 8,598	46. 15,591 + 6,969	47. 36,412 + 8,998	48. 31,942 + 9,689
49. 25,326 + 8,989	50. 16,713 + 9,699	51. 41,115 + 9,995	52. 98,821 + 8,489
53. 51,239 + 9,993	54. 52,913 + 8,297	55. 21,672 + 9,739	56. 29,152 + 5,998
57. 78,317 + 3,993	58. 25,769 + 6,573	59. 71,723 + 9,487	60. 91,851 + 9,969

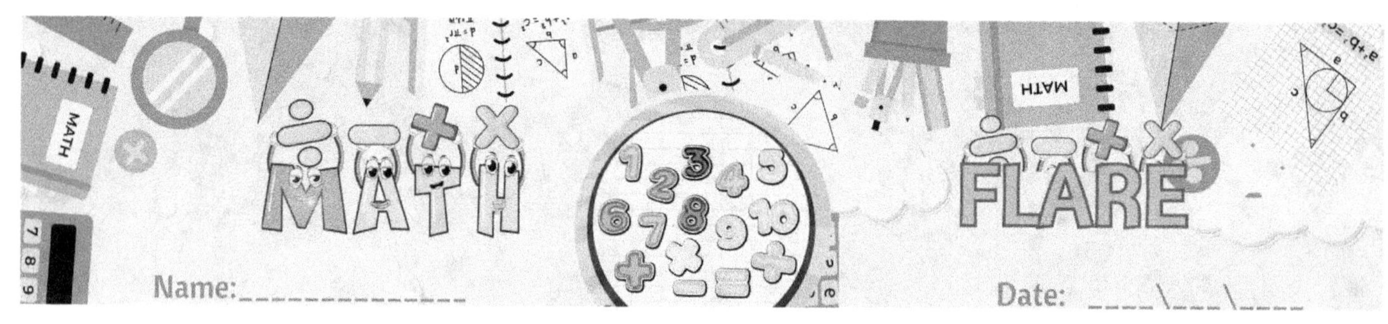

61. 65,731 + 7,889	62. 33,149 + 8,984	63. 89,791 + 5,419	64. 86,125 + 6,999
65. 17,115 + 6,996	66. 31,497 + 9,823	67. 64,512 + 6,799	68. 29,915 + 2,399
69. 65,116 + 7,997	70. 64,699 + 9,762	71. 59,671 + 9,699	72. 76,442 + 8,888
73. 61,992 + 9,218	74. 51,759 + 9,558	75. 98,242 + 6,898	76. 15,589 + 8,653
77. 98,751 + 8,559	78. 71,763 + 9,549	79. 59,789 + 8,897	80. 94,342 + 9,998

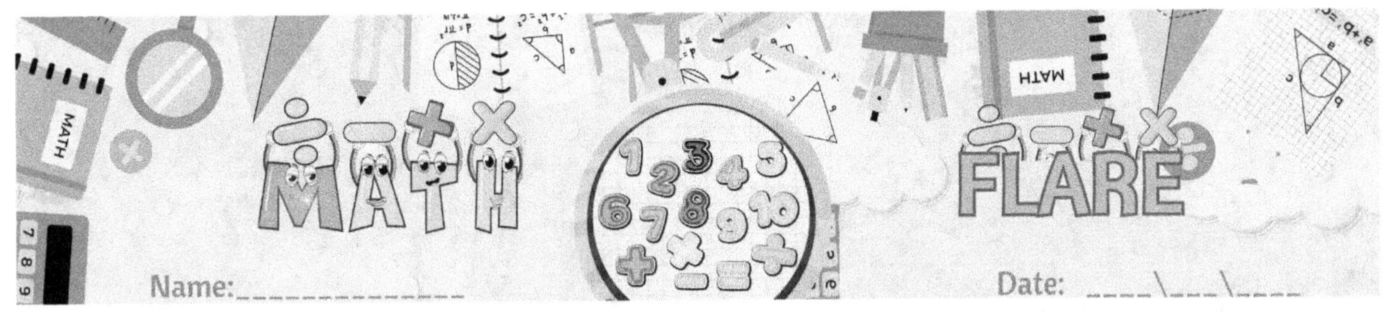

81. 98,511 + 3,899	82. 94,915 + 9,695	83. 56,864 + 4,798	84. 88,939 + 2,589
85. 81,912 + 9,198	86. 11,121 + 9,989	87. 41,121 + 9,989	88. 71,484 + 9,878
89. 12,166 + 9,949	90. 64,845 + 6,765	91. 12,374 + 9,947	92. 31,951 + 9,169
93. 58,656 + 9,998	94. 82,482 + 8,899	95. 91,947 + 9,773	96. 64,113 + 8,997
97. 85,135 + 6,989	98. 99,121 + 3,999	99. 12,143 + 8,978	100. 33,687 + 8,747

Subtraction with Regrouping

Find the difference.

101.	73,185 − 3,696	102.	54,670 − 9,986	103.	65,882 − 2,994	104.	90,384 − 1,597
105.	24,073 − 1,198	106.	60,228 − 1,799	107.	28,137 − 6,668	108.	93,731 − 4,857
109.	10,758 − 5,979	110.	97,767 − 5,888	111.	65,433 − 1,998	112.	33,648 − 2,969
113.	47,871 − 2,999	114.	16,110 − 7,852	115.	94,083 − 4,496	116.	66,738 − 8,889

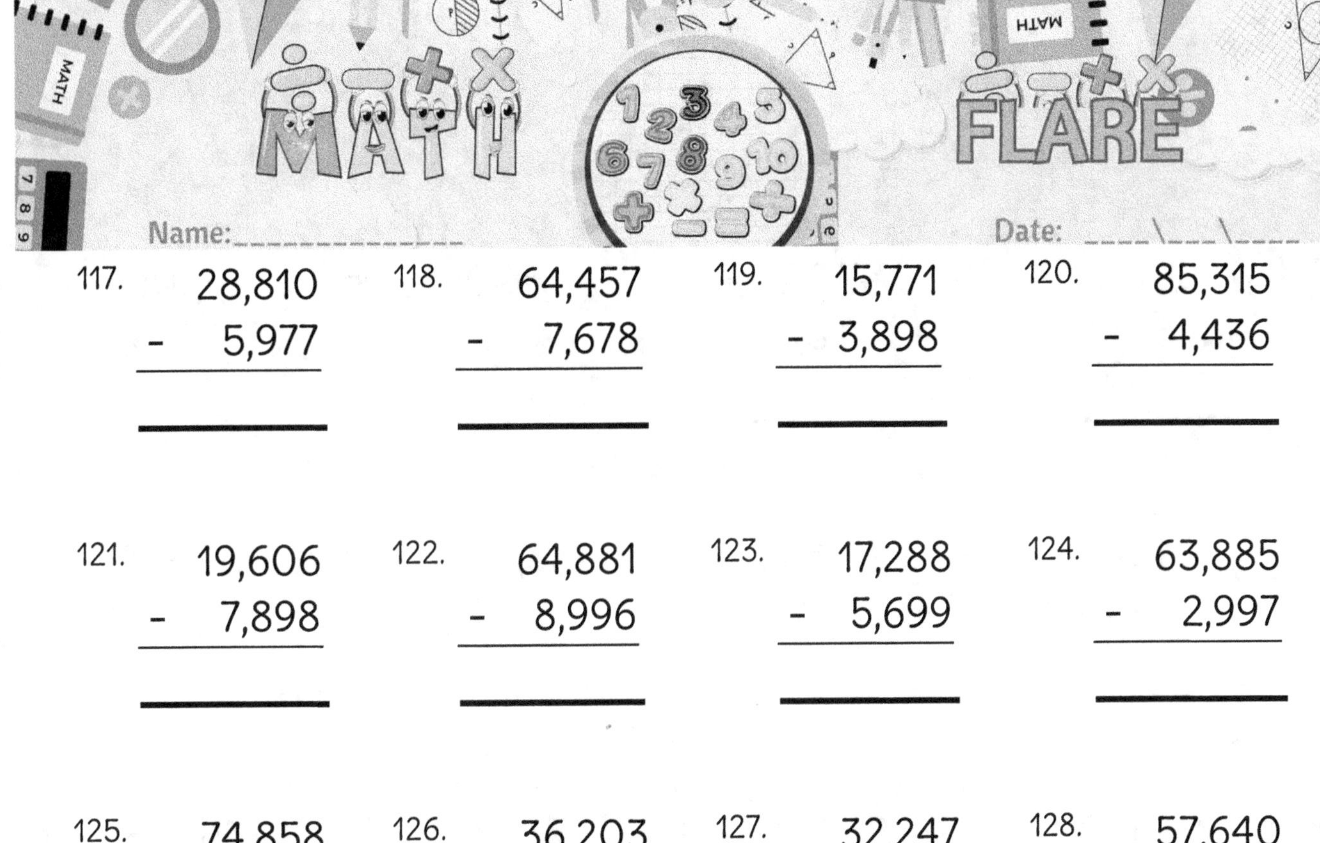

117. 28,810 − 5,977	118. 64,457 − 7,678	119. 15,771 − 3,898	120. 85,315 − 4,436
121. 19,606 − 7,898	122. 64,881 − 8,996	123. 17,288 − 5,699	124. 63,885 − 2,997
125. 74,858 − 6,999	126. 36,203 − 5,835	127. 32,247 − 7,689	128. 57,640 − 6,781
129. 12,515 − 4,627	130. 58,284 − 4,799	131. 18,233 − 2,886	132. 21,438 − 7,959
133. 45,240 − 7,877	134. 88,478 − 7,689	135. 12,231 − 2,752	136. 42,288 − 7,599

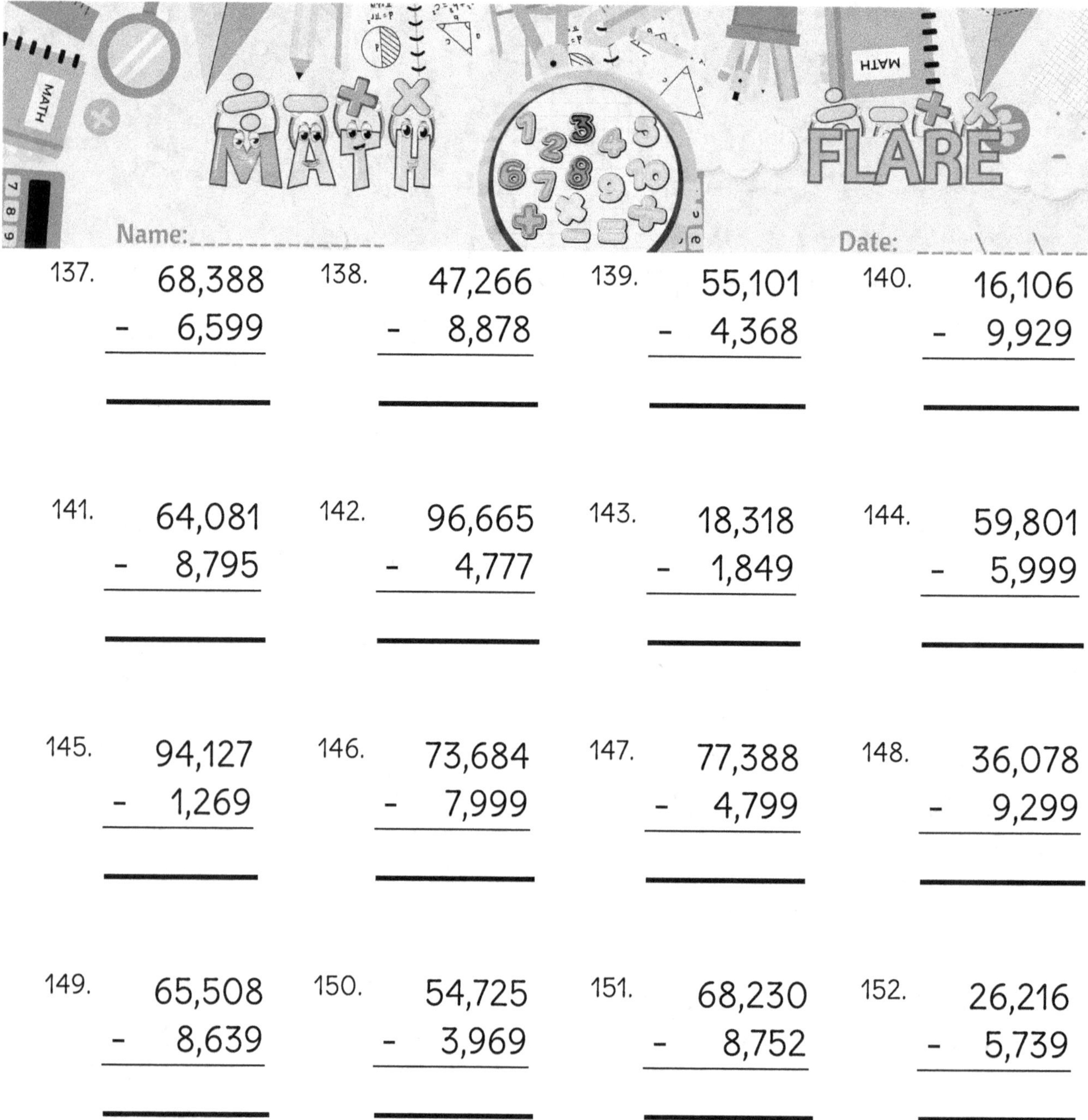

137. 68,388 − 6,599	138. 47,266 − 8,878	139. 55,101 − 4,368	140. 16,106 − 9,929
141. 64,081 − 8,795	142. 96,665 − 4,777	143. 18,318 − 1,849	144. 59,801 − 5,999
145. 94,127 − 1,269	146. 73,684 − 7,999	147. 77,388 − 4,799	148. 36,078 − 9,299
149. 65,508 − 8,639	150. 54,725 − 3,969	151. 68,230 − 8,752	152. 26,216 − 5,739
153. 28,752 − 6,985	154. 89,846 − 6,979	155. 39,548 − 6,999	156. 18,110 − 6,883

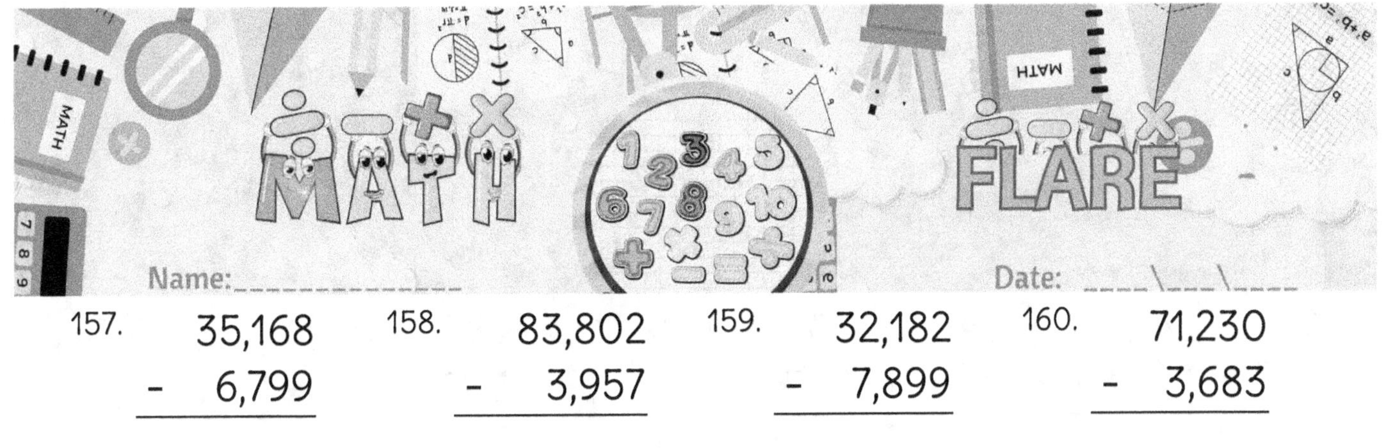

157. 35,168 − 6,799	158. 83,802 − 3,957	159. 32,182 − 7,899	160. 71,230 − 3,683
161. 28,178 − 4,689	162. 82,237 − 1,698	163. 53,826 − 6,988	164. 97,682 − 3,897
165. 37,375 − 5,699	166. 32,875 − 6,996	167. 88,853 − 7,989	168. 33,028 − 7,659
169. 71,445 − 4,976	170. 24,280 − 5,798	171. 28,455 − 9,768	172. 22,448 − 3,799
173. 93,135 − 1,486	174. 49,324 − 2,535	175. 63,616 − 1,757	176. 68,554 − 8,766

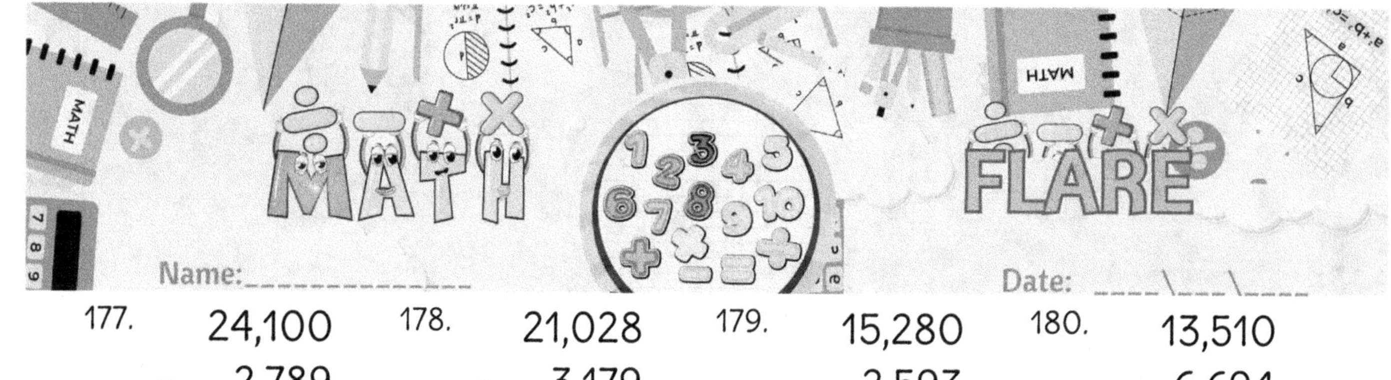

177. 24,100 − 2,789	178. 21,028 − 3,179	179. 15,280 − 2,593	180. 13,510 − 6,694
181. 63,444 − 6,897	182. 41,417 − 8,588	183. 46,178 − 4,899	184. 79,877 − 5,998
185. 44,006 − 1,729	186. 59,123 − 8,285	187. 64,105 − 2,447	188. 18,382 − 3,797
189. 34,036 − 5,768	190. 17,848 − 4,999	191. 28,480 − 8,792	192. 67,348 − 3,689
193. 87,863 − 4,986	194. 55,668 − 7,989	195. 65,868 − 1,989	196. 71,272 − 5,685

Addition Unknown Number

Find the unknown number.

197. 458 + 663 = _______

198. _______ + 594 = 1,531

199. 596 + _______ = 1,590

200. 887 + _______ = 1,434

201. 351 + _______ = 1,330

202. 763 + _______ = 1,331

203. 563 + 858 = _______

204. 331 + 899 = _______

205. 195 + _______ = 1,134

206. 976 + 589 = _______

207. 174 + 948 = _______

208. 424 + _______ = 1,220

209. 116 + _______ = 1,111

210. _______ + 179 = 1,130

211. 926 + _______ = 1,114

212. 923 + _______ = 1,420

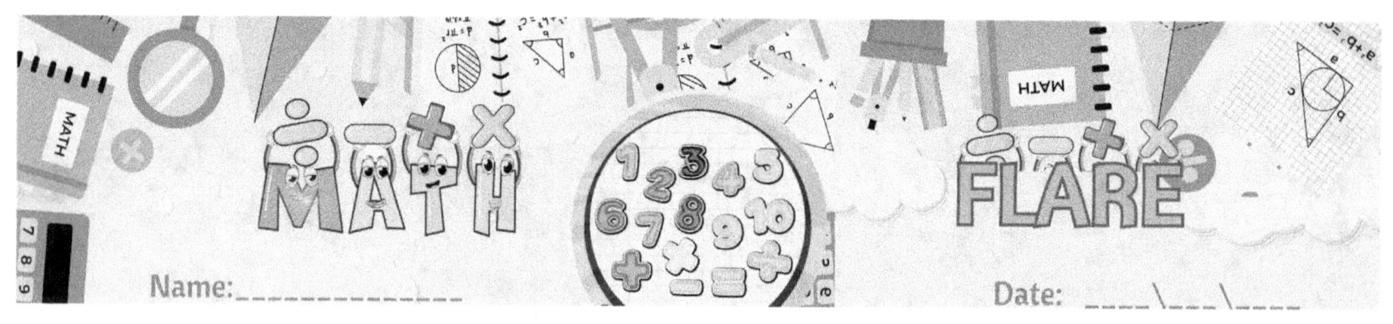

213. 459 + _____ = 1,358

214. _____ + 979 = 1,450

215. _____ + 999 = 1,312

216. 773 + _____ = 1,720

217. _____ + 639 = 1,323

218. 241 + 979 = _____

219. 211 + 899 = _____

220. 754 + 468 = _____

221. 228 + 996 = _____

222. 615 + _____ = 1,513

223. 136 + _____ = 1,131

224. _____ + 882 = 1,370

225. 319 + _____ = 1,115

226. 578 + 557 = _____

227. 443 + _____ = 1,332

228. _____ + 689 = 1,310

229. _____ + 436 = 1,422

230. 214 + 896 = _____

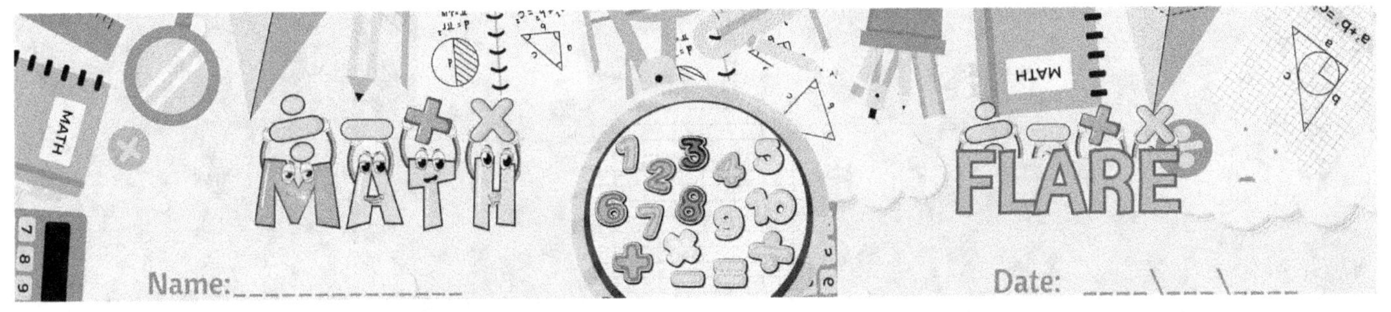

231. 486 + _____ = 1,313

232. _____ + 625 = 1,422

233. 166 + 987 = _____

234. 895 + 546 = _____

235. 515 + _____ = 1,514

236. 651 + 989 = _____

237. 441 + _____ = 1,440

238. 874 + 479 = _____

239. _____ + 538 = 1,110

240. 391 + 829 = _____

241. _____ + 699 = 1,340

242. 798 + 927 = _____

243. 111 + 999 = _____

244. 612 + 799 = _____

245. 119 + _____ = 1,116

246. 387 + 773 = _____

247. 116 + _____ = 1,110

248. 636 + _____ = 1,611

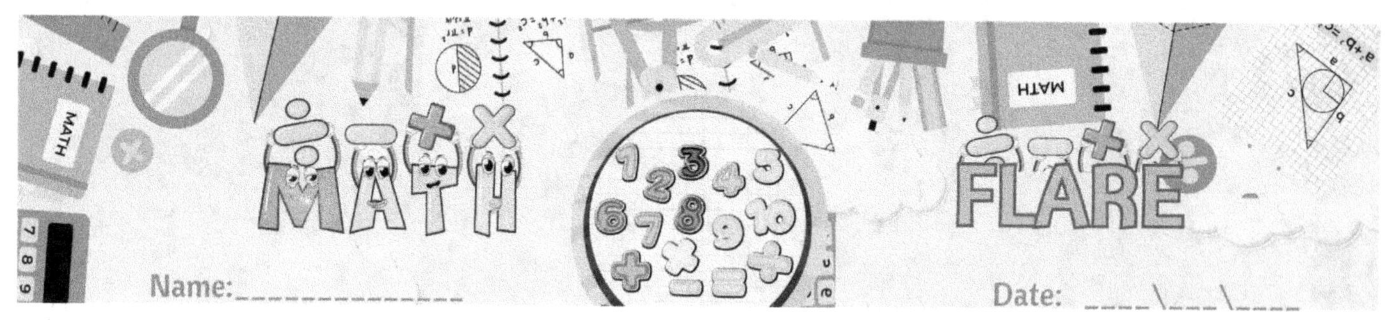

Name:________________   Date: ____________

249. _______ + 795 = 1,553

250. 753 + 987 = _______

251. _______ + 974 = 1,311

252. _______ + 998 = 1,415

253. 624 + _______ = 1,310

254. 161 + _______ = 1,160

255. 689 + _______ = 1,570

256. 145 + 976 = _______

257. _______ + 828 = 1,721

258. 523 + _______ = 1,311

259. 595 + _______ = 1,391

260. 528 + _______ = 1,124

261. 534 + _______ = 1,131

262. 762 + 878 = _______

263. _______ + 299 = 1,210

264. 391 + 969 = _______

265. 711 + _______ = 1,310

266. 451 + _______ = 1,140

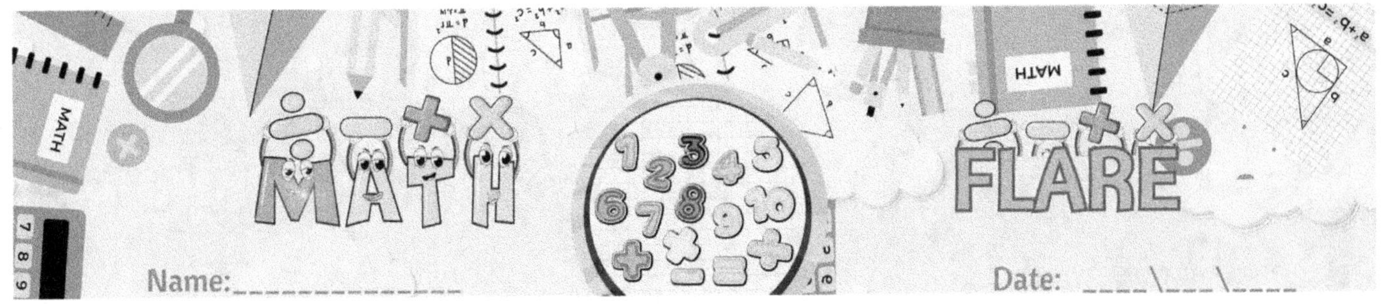

267. 989 + 695 = _______

268. 351 + _______ = 1,220

269. 511 + 999 = _______

270. _______ + 899 = 1,210

271. 789 + 858 = _______

272. 389 + _______ = 1,375

273. 728 + _______ = 1,517

274. 426 + 897 = _______

275. 482 + 988 = _______

276. _______ + 999 = 1,513

277. 576 + 545 = _______

278. 511 + 899 = _______

279. 495 + 746 = _______

280. 771 + _______ = 1,710

281. 224 + _______ = 1,113

282. _______ + 586 = 1,124

283. 531 + 779 = _______

284. 886 + _______ = 1,184

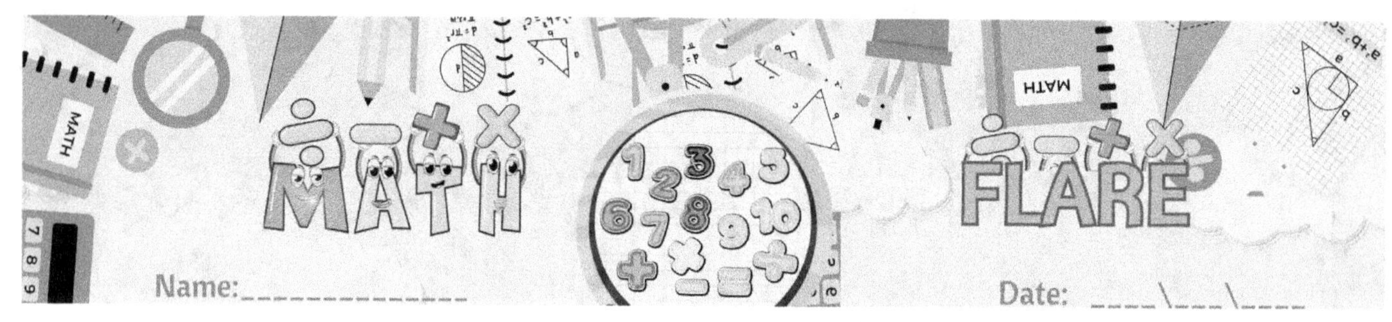

285. 578 + _____ = 1,460

286. 369 + _____ = 1,126

287. 581 + _____ = 1,130

288. _____ + 695 = 1,111

289. 238 + _____ = 1,224

290. 249 + _____ = 1,220

291. 794 + 589 = _____

292. 585 + 725 = _____

293. _____ + 991 = 1,140

294. 819 + 898 = _____

295. 285 + _____ = 1,264

296. 245 + _____ = 1,242

297. 667 + _____ = 1,341

298. _____ + 748 = 1,710

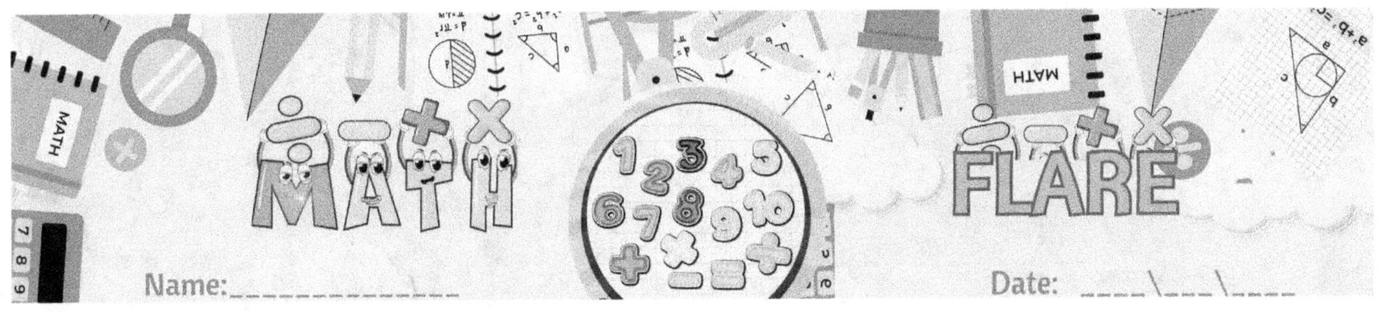

Subtraction: Unknown Number

Find the unknown number.

299. _____ − 158 = 262

300. _____ − 947 = 28

301. _____ − 134 = 208

302. _____ − 227 = 102

303. 718 − _____ = 441

304. 478 − 157 = _____

305. _____ − 701 = 134

306. 740 − _____ = 541

307. 598 − _____ = 1

308. 245 − _____ = 58

309. 555 − 461 = _____

310. 177 − _____ = 74

311. _____ − 135 = 812

312. 113 − _____ = 11

313. 737 − 464 = _____

314. _____ − 214 = 374

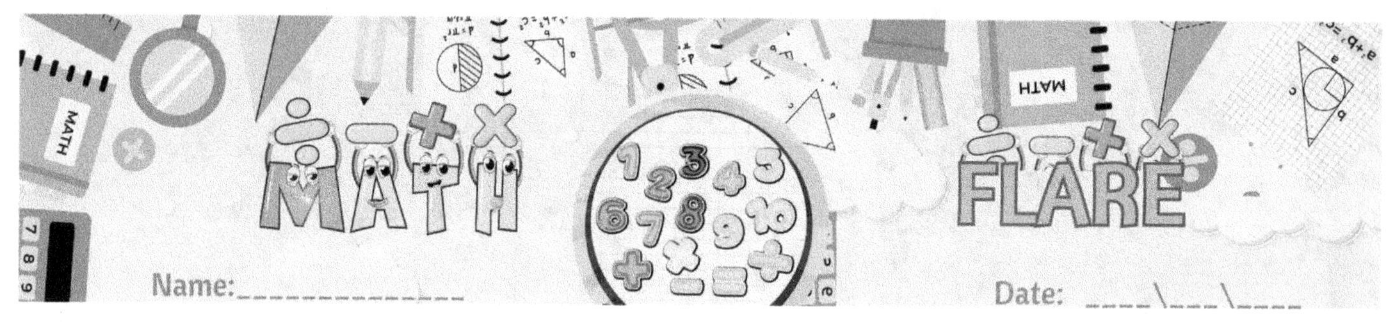

315. 478 - 334 = _____

316. 355 - _____ = 7

317. 380 - 155 = _____

318. 529 - 370 = _____

319. _____ - 351 = 4

320. _____ - 105 = 1

321. 113 - 108 = _____

322. 114 - _____ = 9

323. 729 - 104 = _____

324. 256 - _____ = 57

325. 226 - _____ = 81

326. 292 - 208 = _____

327. _____ - 179 = 6

328. 123 - 105 = _____

329. 215 - _____ = 99

330. _____ - 188 = 673

331. 768 - _____ = 543

332. 756 - _____ = 527

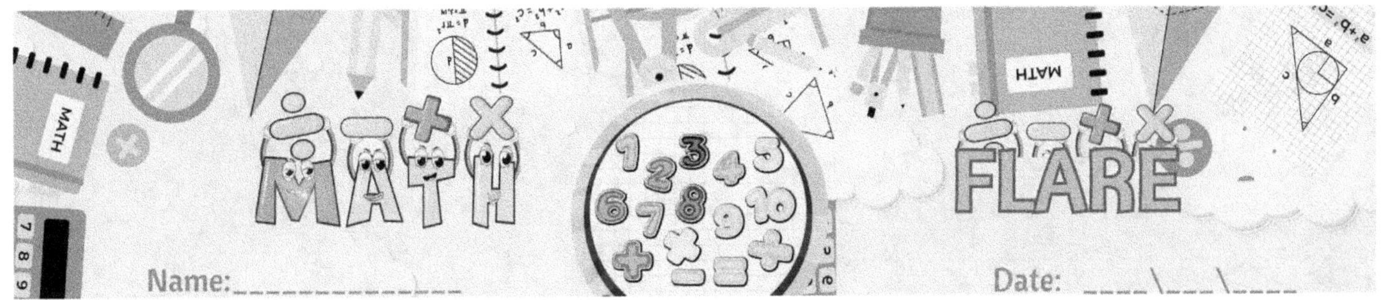

333. 580 - _____ = 125

334. 858 - _____ = 488

335. 568 - _____ = 219

336. 384 - _____ = 136

337. 807 - _____ = 482

338. _____ - 108 = 17

339. _____ - 115 = 9

340. _____ - 365 = 112

341. 458 - 426 = _____

342. _____ - 105 = 79

343. 465 - _____ = 102

344. 890 - 401 = _____

345. _____ - 139 = 116

346. 551 - _____ = 384

347. _____ - 211 = 13

348. _____ - 119 = 4

349. 917 - 768 = _____

350. 869 - 839 = _____

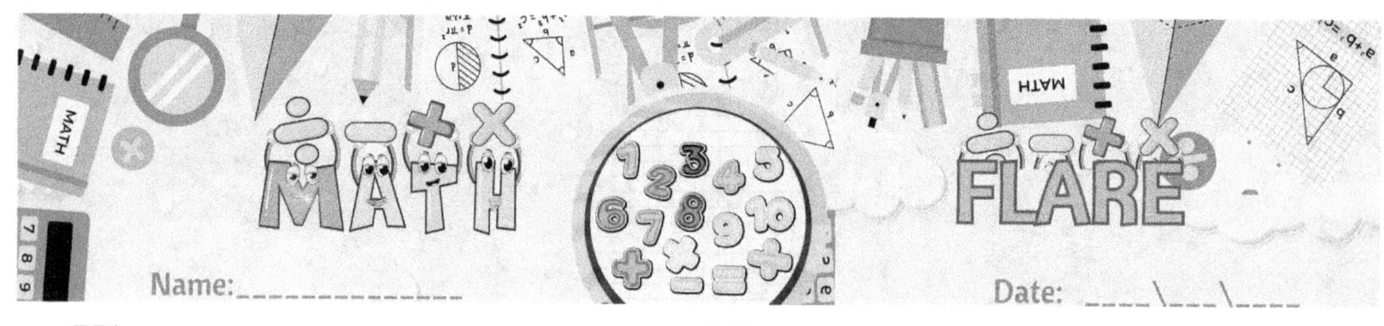

351. 247 - 220 = _____

352. 200 - _____ = 39

353. _____ - 127 = 12

354. 797 - 641 = _____

355. _____ - 687 = 225

356. 281 - _____ = 90

357. _____ - 193 = 551

358. 745 - 636 = _____

359. _____ - 156 = 28

360. _____ - 677 = 134

361. _____ - 458 = 416

362. 265 - _____ = 120

363. _____ - 105 = 22

364. 445 - _____ = 36

365. 363 - 152 = _____

366. 455 - _____ = 281

367. 794 - 418 = _____

368. 585 - _____ = 204

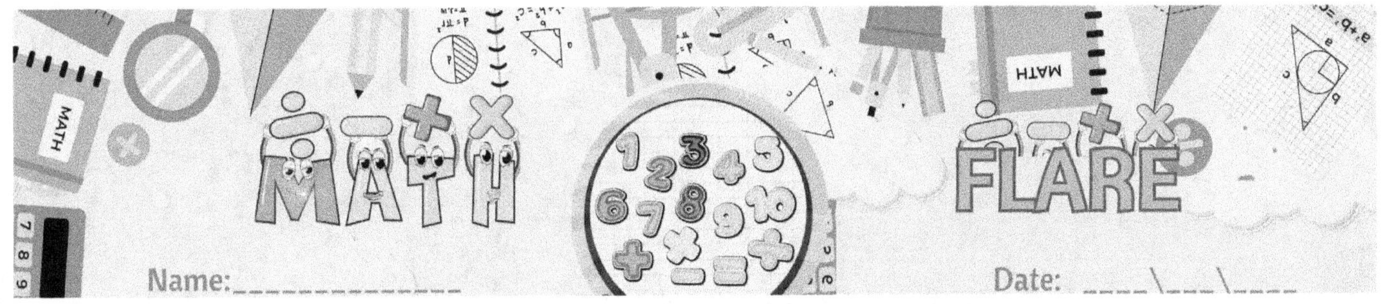

369. 819 - _____ = 370

370. 116 - _____ = 5

371. 950 - 186 = _____

372. 529 - _____ = 236

373. 145 - 100 = _____

374. 488 - 486 = _____

375. 257 - _____ = 127

376. 760 - 258 = _____

377. _____ - 101 = 23

378. _____ - 163 = 27

379. 670 - _____ = 91

380. _____ - 555 = 65

381. 377 - 344 = _____

382. _____ - 406 = 129

383. _____ - 393 = 2

384. 756 - _____ = 487

385. 644 - _____ = 470

386. _____ - 117 = 11

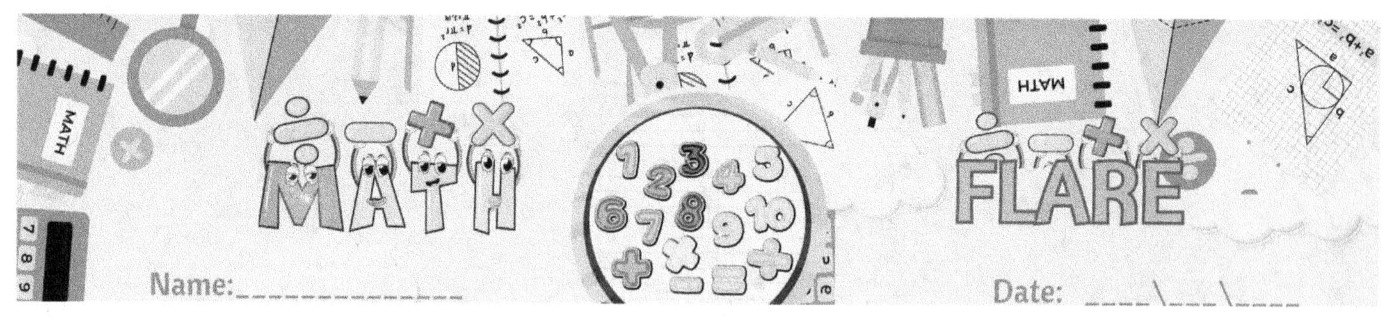

387. 686 - _____ = 541

388. 879 - _____ = 188

389. _____ - 751 = 235

390. _____ - 106 = 193

391. 763 - _____ = 405

392. 748 - 164 = _____

393. 518 - 165 = _____

394. 263 - 219 = _____

395. 422 - 370 = _____

396. _____ - 917 = 34

397. _____ - 217 = 698

398. 465 - 124 = _____

399. _____ - 529 = 126

400. 209 - _____ = 103

401. 344 - _____ = 202

402. 451 - _____ = 338

403. 246 - 118 = _____

404. _____ - 602 = 26

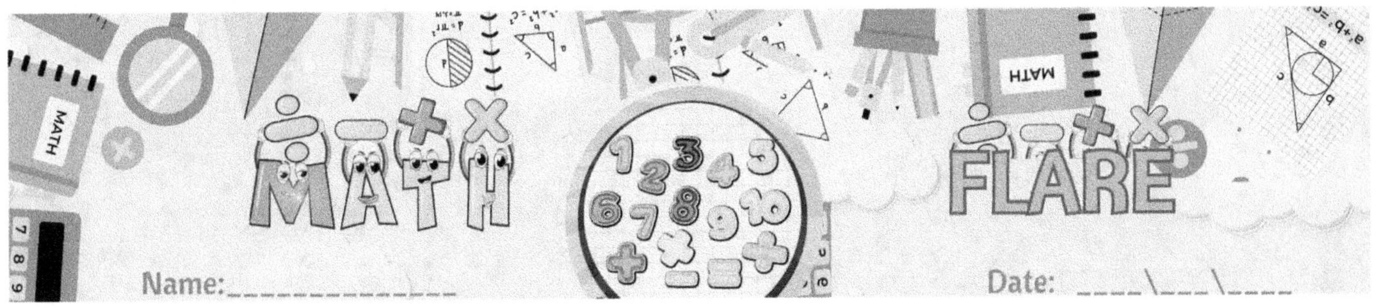

Addition (3 Addends)

Find the sum.

405.
```
   4,004
   7,630
+  8,470
_______
```

406.
```
   5,358
   9,904
+  9,965
_______
```

407.
```
   8,260
   3,610
+  9,200
_______
```

408.
```
   7,953
   8,626
+  7,183
_______
```

409.
```
   2,078
   4,782
+  3,224
_______
```

410.
```
   6,753
   5,250
+  7,280
_______
```

411.
```
   8,872
   1,093
+  1,149
_______
```

412.
```
   3,541
   2,446
+  8,760
_______
```

413.
```
   9,262
   7,831
+  4,208
_______
```

414.
```
   1,098
   3,959
+  1,949
_______
```

415.
```
   5,497
   4,711
+  2,555
_______
```

416.
```
   6,485
   3,185
+  6,134
_______
```

417.
```
   5,970
   3,395
+  6,351
_______
```

418.
```
   2,104
   8,845
+  1,751
_______
```

419.
```
   1,705
   3,446
+  6,538
_______
```

420.
```
   6,338
   8,569
+  5,702
_______
```

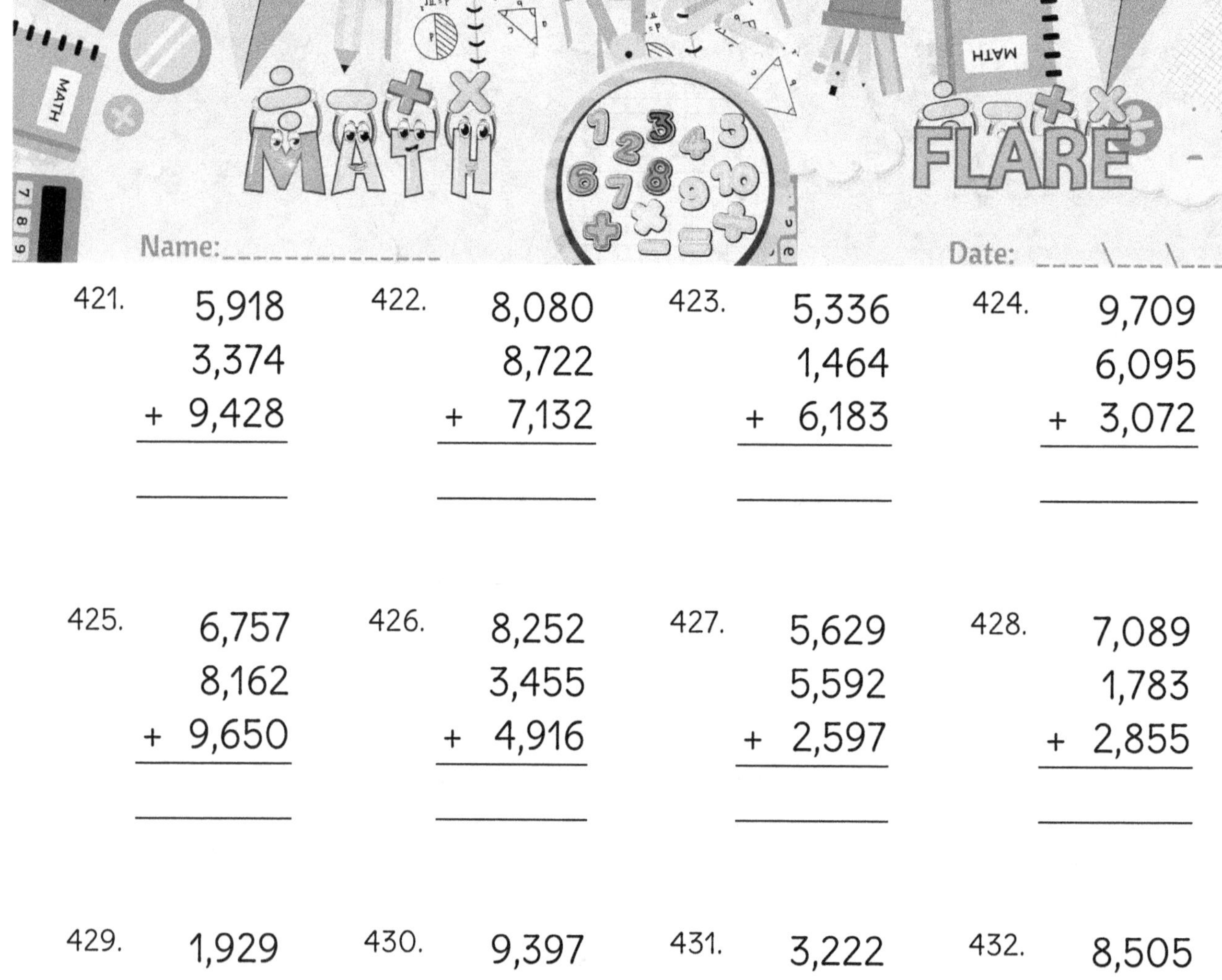

421. 5,918 3,374 + 9,428	422. 8,080 8,722 + 7,132	423. 5,336 1,464 + 6,183	424. 9,709 6,095 + 3,072
425. 6,757 8,162 + 9,650	426. 8,252 3,455 + 4,916	427. 5,629 5,592 + 2,597	428. 7,089 1,783 + 2,855
429. 1,929 7,768 + 2,247	430. 9,397 2,835 + 8,999	431. 3,222 3,924 + 9,261	432. 8,505 5,179 + 1,585
433. 2,520 7,416 + 5,987	434. 5,422 2,149 + 2,721	435. 9,950 6,260 + 7,299	436. 4,279 5,346 + 1,683

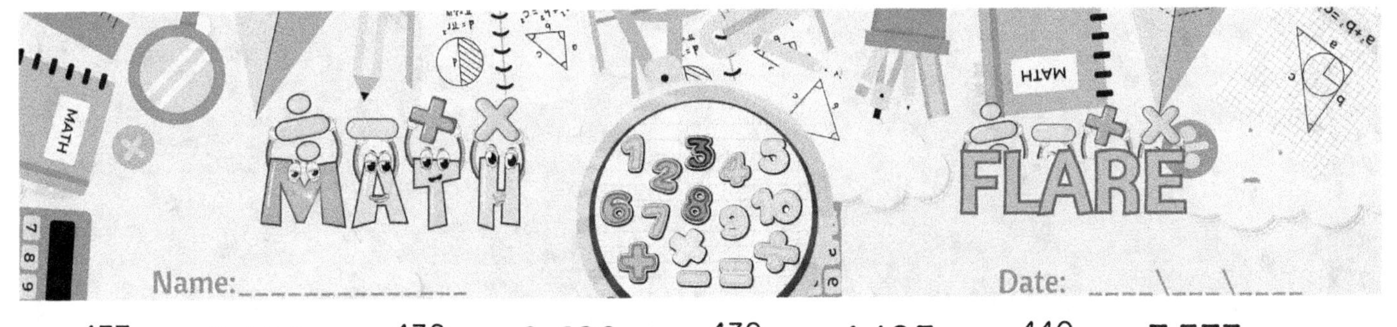

437. 2,100 3,453 + 9,990	438. 2,622 1,709 + 3,977	439. 4,105 8,828 + 2,591	440. 7,573 7,151 + 1,954
441. 5,885 5,938 + 8,627	442. 7,184 7,487 + 3,171	443. 3,810 8,251 + 3,983	444. 9,065 6,732 + 6,038
445. 8,928 1,207 + 4,443	446. 9,875 7,138 + 5,522	447. 5,555 7,649 + 3,422	448. 1,564 8,298 + 9,382
449. 9,008 1,600 + 3,215	450. 6,285 5,400 + 6,350	451. 8,993 4,946 + 1,266	452. 5,033 9,536 + 6,210

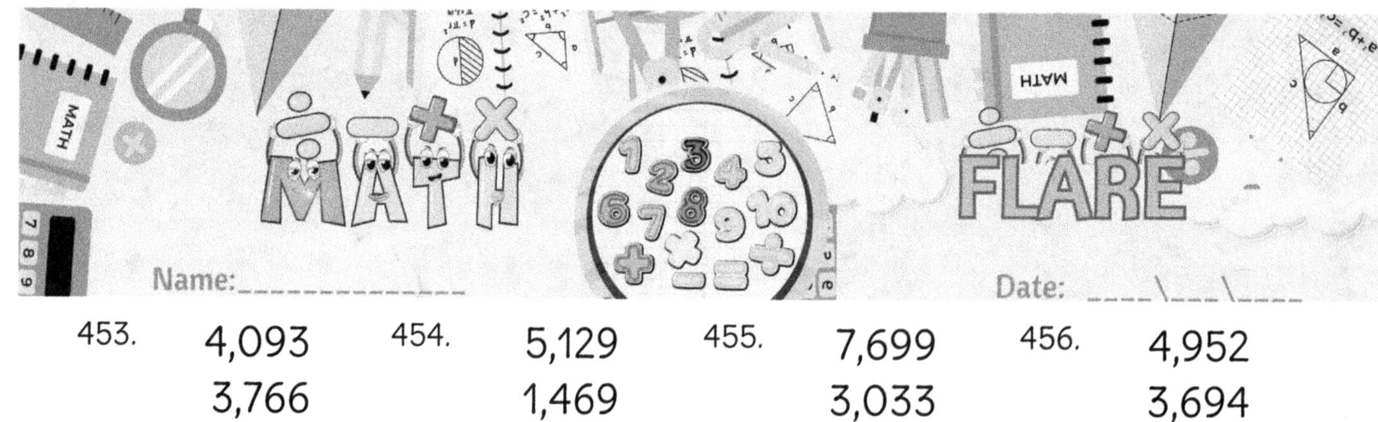

453. 4,093 3,766 + 8,773	454. 5,129 1,469 + 7,094	455. 7,699 3,033 + 6,720	456. 4,952 3,694 + 1,503
457. 9,532 4,229 + 2,690	458. 7,068 3,018 + 9,500	459. 8,531 5,321 + 7,639	460. 9,244 8,175 + 6,887
461. 9,955 7,524 + 3,851	462. 7,631 1,072 + 2,786	463. 5,772 4,895 + 1,669	464. 8,232 6,782 + 4,372
465. 6,748 1,426 + 7,181	466. 6,327 3,864 + 6,264	467. 3,662 5,056 + 7,906	468. 2,712 6,752 + 2,171

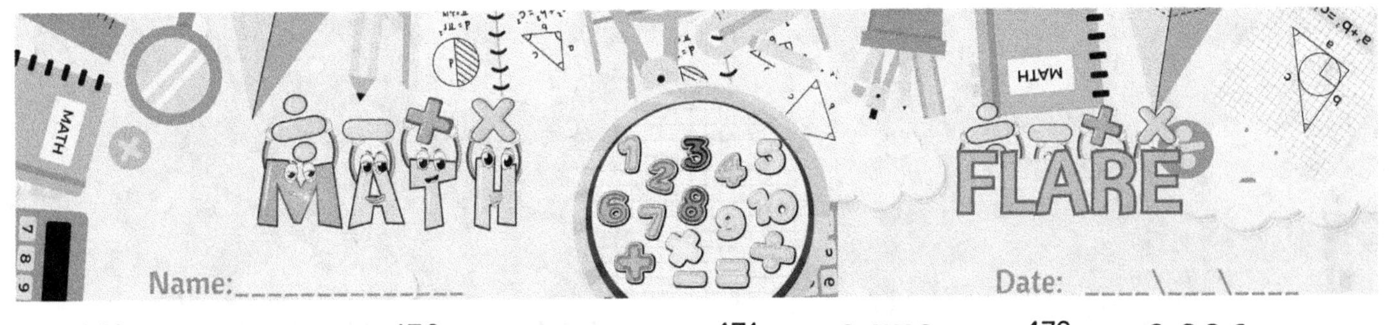

469.   4,660
     2,925
+ 2,928
____

470.   1,764
     6,501
+ 5,216
____

471.   8,570
     4,848
+ 5,590
____

472.   2,886
     5,173
+ 3,944
____

473.   4,243
     1,068
+ 2,961
____

474.   4,934
     9,179
+ 8,798
____

475.   9,833
     2,300
+ 7,447
____

476.   8,318
     1,320
+ 2,592
____

477.   3,320
     3,204
+ 2,457
____

478.   2,375
     6,582
+ 4,119
____

479.   8,980
     8,242
+ 1,772
____

480.   2,681
     3,972
+ 8,147
____

481.   9,856
     5,008
+ 8,393
____

482.   6,453
     9,661
+ 2,934
____

483.   8,781
     4,862
+ 6,252
____

484.   4,237
     3,085
+ 3,796
____

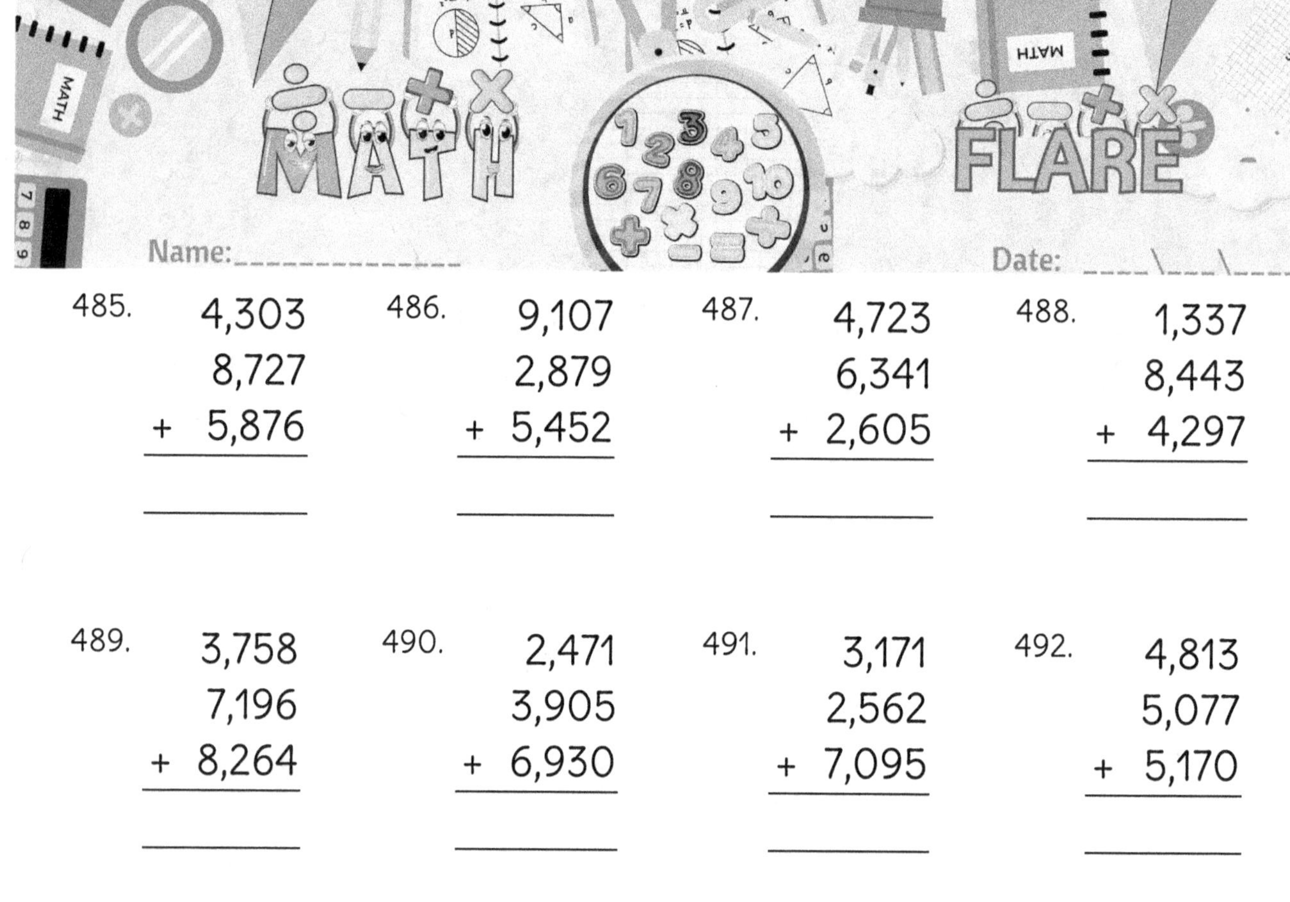

485.   4,303
       8,727
   + 5,876

486.   9,107
       2,879
   + 5,452

487.   4,723
       6,341
   + 2,605

488.   1,337
       8,443
   + 4,297

489.   3,758
       7,196
   + 8,264

490.   2,471
       3,905
   + 6,930

491.   3,171
       2,562
   + 7,095

492.   4,813
       5,077
   + 5,170

493.   1,405
       4,380
   + 2,637

494.   5,513
       9,536
   + 6,457

495.   6,339
       9,081
   + 1,119

496.   8,660
       8,070
   + 7,855

497.   8,242
       9,872
   + 6,364

498.   6,319
       7,957
   + 7,630

499.   6,542
       9,519
   + 6,564

500.   5,097
       3,694
   + 3,466

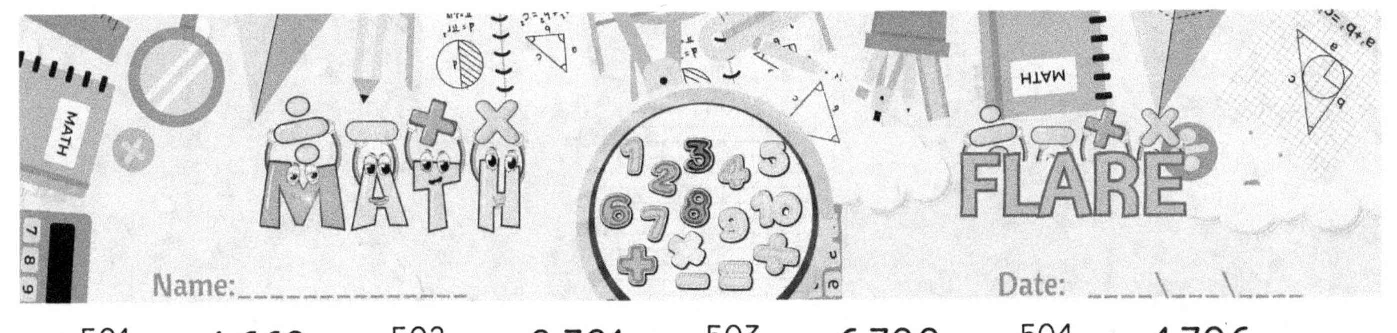

501.
4,668
7,310
+ 1,957
____

502.
9,321
2,066
+ 1,523
____

503.
6,700
9,489
+ 4,650
____

504.
1,706
8,702
+ 8,498
____

505.
3,815
9,209
+ 6,804
____

506.
6,147
4,997
+ 9,361
____

507.
4,178
5,097
+ 9,124
____

508.
1,410
4,227
+ 4,032
____

509.
1,566
6,851
+ 4,604
____

510.
9,464
8,270
+ 5,556
____

511.
8,605
6,307
+ 1,686
____

512.
9,171
1,845
+ 3,225
____

513.
5,500
7,016
+ 8,015
____

514.
9,595
2,961
+ 8,580
____

515.
4,204
7,536
+ 2,170
____

516.
7,865
3,504
+ 8,747
____

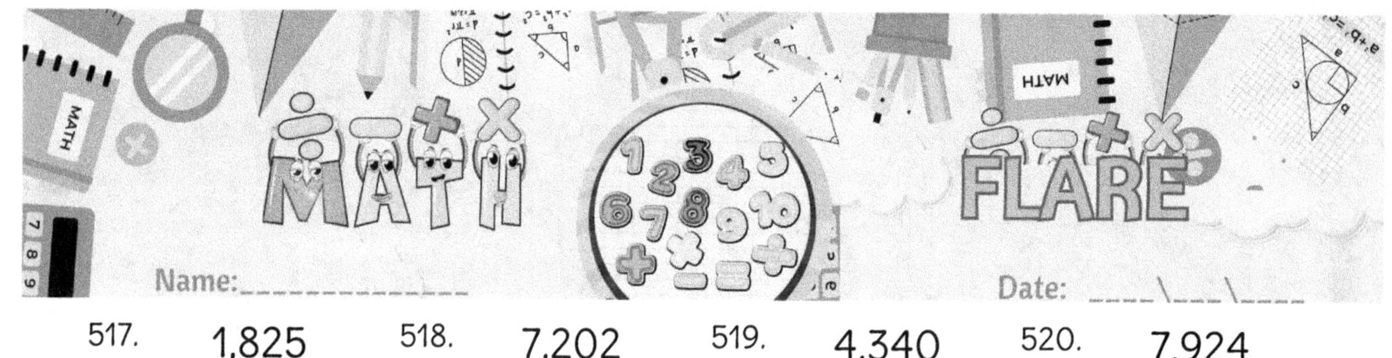

517. 1,825 1,396 + 5,522	518. 7,202 1,919 + 8,596	519. 4,340 4,259 + 4,083	520. 7,924 8,755 + 5,214
521. 6,918 7,235 + 2,219	522. 9,093 3,100 + 3,395	523. 7,812 4,643 + 8,364	524. 4,579 1,647 + 7,980
525. 2,346 4,582 + 3,136	526. 1,544 7,204 + 6,690	527. 2,863 3,700 + 4,346	528. 5,856 8,639 + 7,875
529. 1,034 2,403 + 5,388	530. 3,089 5,830 + 7,585	531. 9,141 7,575 + 8,260	532. 3,801 3,677 + 5,725

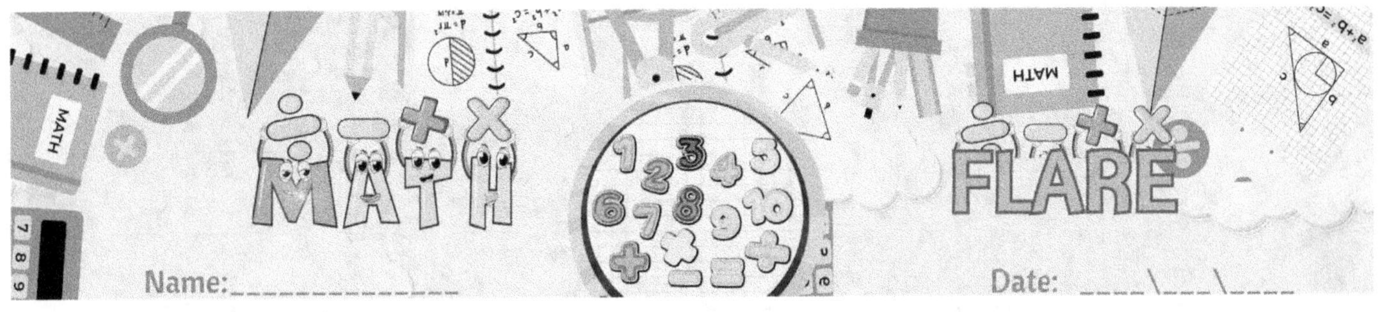

Multiple Operations: Addition Subtraction

Find the sum.

533.
```
   99,560
   39,437
-  31,968
-  15,369
_________
```

534.
```
   63,464
   81,752
-  19,388
-  31,741
_________
```

535.
```
   99,512
   54,647
-  43,025
-  32,856
_________
```

536.
```
   55,178
-  34,710
-  19,696
   79,783
_________
```

537.
```
   93,098
-  43,883
-  13,440
   92,117
_________
```

538.
```
   93,339
   80,107
-  54,999
-  12,376
_________
```

539.
```
   91,119
   48,525
-  10,976
-  34,778
_________
```

540.
```
   68,603
-  19,170
   73,238
-  46,127
_________
```

541.
```
   67,397
-  36,185
   41,194
-  18,655
_________
```

542.
```
   65,942
   84,325
-  23,442
-  20,327
_________
```

543.
```
   76,994
-  31,514
   23,942
-  14,542
_________
```

544.
```
   82,508
-  41,688
-  10,176
   72,382
_________
```

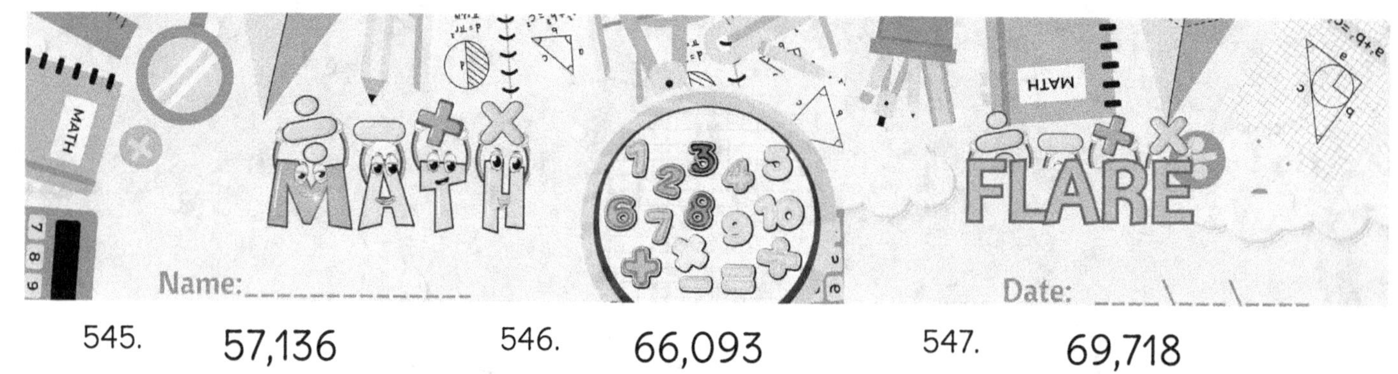

545.   57,136
    20,816
− 21,502
− 34,193
	546. 66,093
	− 13,485
	− 12,503
	   29,014
		547. 69,718
		   49,183
		− 24,249
		− 44,202

548.   89,899
− 39,610
− 17,285
   80,685
	549. 90,704
	   93,795
	− 20,457
	− 28,994
		550. 64,112
		   76,049
		− 33,948
		− 10,936

551.   75,440
   87,240
− 29,063
− 26,824
	552. 83,082
	− 50,457
	− 19,989
	   18,862
		553. 74,004
		   39,570
		− 32,640
		− 18,196

554.   97,668
   24,850
− 35,033
− 18,913
	555. 78,540
	   22,179
	− 48,936
	− 43,753
		556. 77,912
		− 34,240
		   50,854
		− 47,385

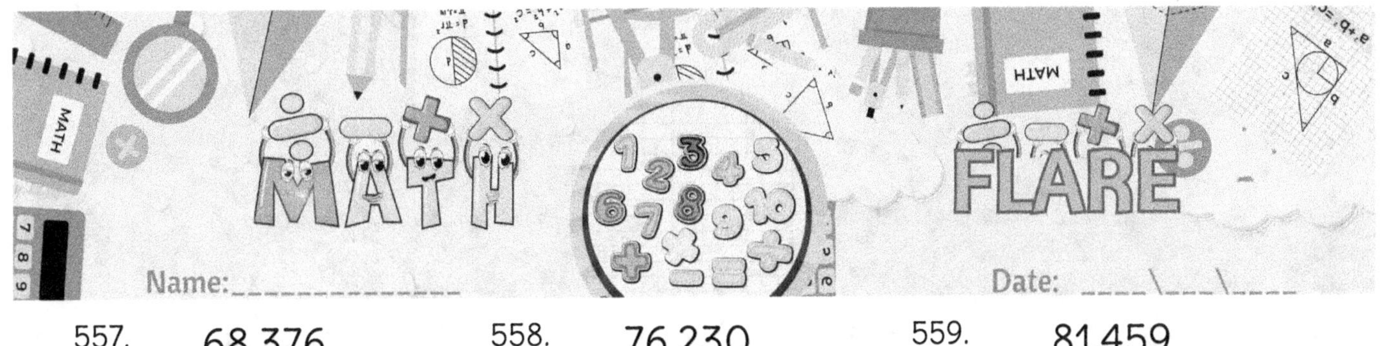

557.	68,376	558.	76,230	559.	81,459
	43,257		- 36,263		- 20,565
	- 23,837		- 24,703		- 13,753
	- 40,611		38,225		44,946

560.	84,421	561.	99,723	562.	61,968
	71,639		- 19,818		- 54,940
	- 36,424		- 25,197		85,349
	- 29,262		50,229		- 38,279

563.	71,863	564.	94,088	565.	73,192
	13,089		75,193		- 36,678
	- 50,453		- 33,022		16,894
	- 11,645		- 51,200		- 21,048

566.	81,619	567.	92,706	568.	58,671
	- 44,256		- 18,527		25,120
	66,401		63,473		- 34,491
	- 47,741		- 42,102		- 42,943

569. 79,664
− 29,673
− 42,551
   36,188
	570. 64,042
	   10,625
	− 40,415
	− 17,241
		571. 78,953
		   71,117
		− 23,747
		− 29,686

572. 85,810
   48,110
− 30,024
− 48,862
	573. 87,542
	   25,105
	− 54,280
	− 12,743
		574. 82,372
		− 24,970
		   85,285
		− 20,466

575. 81,617
   54,911
− 37,407
− 53,441
	576. 73,203
	− 15,572
	   59,213
	− 19,303
		577. 77,052
		− 12,732
		− 33,358
		   48,829

578. 95,968
− 19,928
   74,313
− 27,880
	579. 96,262
	− 45,010
	− 39,793
	   92,121
		580. 75,509
		− 18,514
		   23,862
		− 28,651

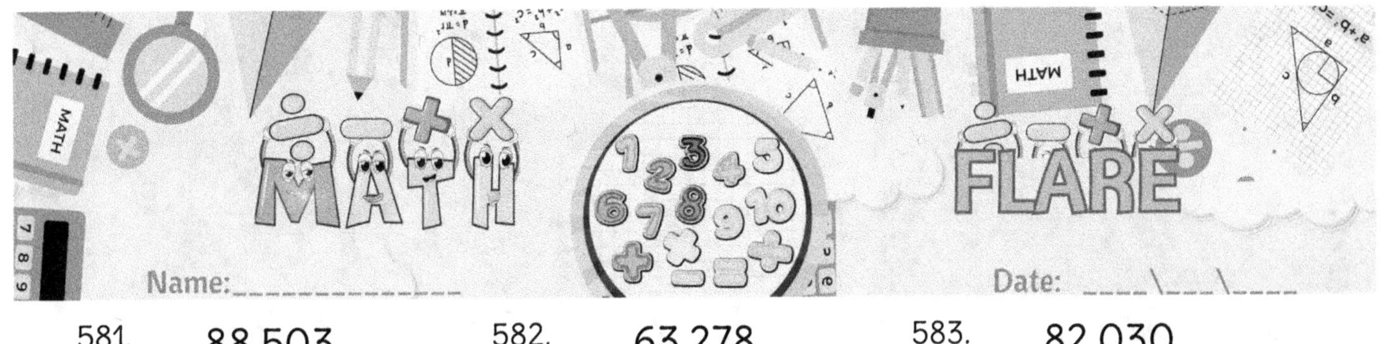

581.	88,503	582.	63,278	583.	82,030
	75,748		53,494		62,322
	− 54,559		− 20,348		− 41,476
	− 51,119		− 19,694		− 41,587

584.	72,904	585.	60,950	586.	95,697
	− 41,973		− 14,443		− 10,609
	90,466		− 44,587		95,787
	− 28,381		66,156		− 32,614

587.	75,395	588.	82,470	589.	70,523
	62,800		− 51,582		27,511
	− 16,481		− 26,226		− 19,938
	− 47,362		46,207		− 40,329

590.	61,012	591.	92,383	592.	78,451
	− 38,487		37,327		− 10,568
	− 10,285		− 47,383		99,950
	10,611		− 24,807		− 19,288

593.	594.	595.
94,777	65,880	89,980
38,237	57,705	53,889
− 45,108	− 32,954	− 30,723
− 26,066	− 42,893	− 36,879

596.	597.	598.
70,265	91,204	77,035
− 27,986	36,744	29,806
− 29,528	− 26,063	− 22,368
70,898	− 19,149	− 32,464

599.	600.	601.
58,418	63,225	81,424
94,653	− 38,085	94,385
− 45,694	98,324	− 52,584
− 37,033	− 29,827	− 23,352

602.	603.	604.
61,472	85,800	62,763
− 28,890	54,088	48,288
24,444	− 50,348	− 40,039
− 46,671	− 39,068	− 29,397

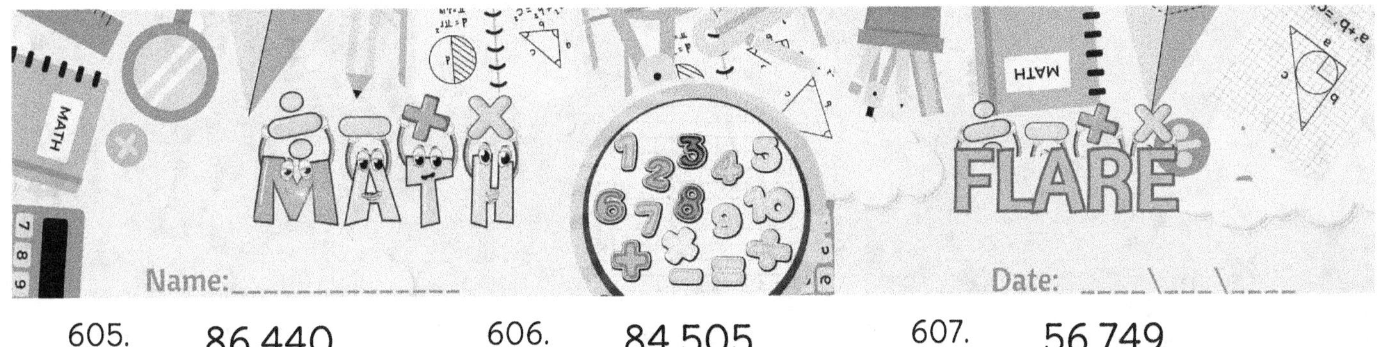

605. 86,440
  23,868
− 33,603
− 20,079
	606. 84,505
	− 45,826
	  74,505
	− 39,873
		607. 56,749
		− 22,644
		− 16,774
		  37,109

608. 88,158
− 50,921
− 24,931
  23,789
	609. 77,781
	  11,792
	− 10,454
	− 28,073
		610. 75,400
		  37,742
		− 33,976
		− 27,313

611. 61,149
− 34,391
  56,696
− 54,991
	612. 69,553
	− 38,299
	− 16,943
	  68,550
		613. 67,286
		− 26,297
		− 37,954
		  12,583

614. 59,481
− 44,082
− 14,238
  81,198
	615. 64,939
	  35,422
	− 21,601
	− 48,828
		616. 61,243
		− 48,667
		  17,026
		− 25,194

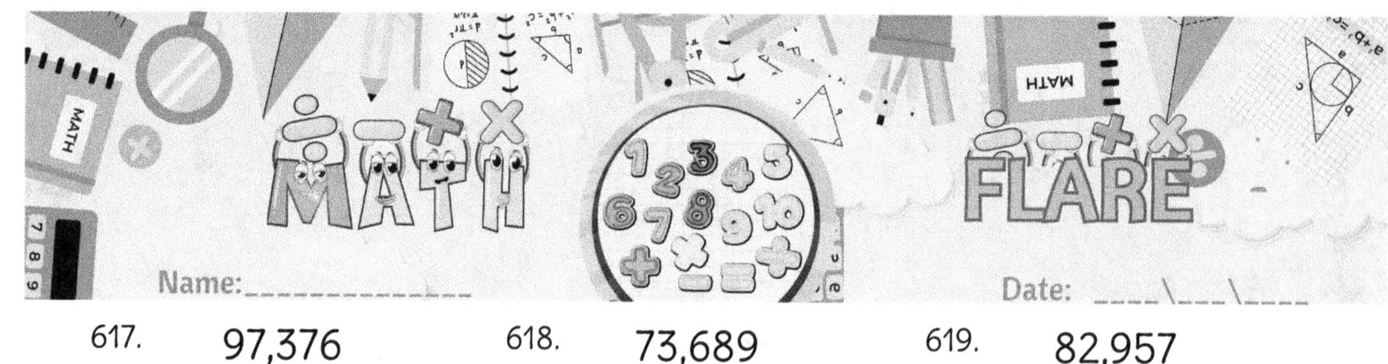

617.	618.	619.
97,376	73,689	82,957
76,908	− 21,966	− 16,289
− 16,286	− 50,793	− 13,929
− 16,868	45,138	20,227

620.	621.	622.
67,477	97,945	55,327
74,521	66,742	− 33,375
− 25,319	− 11,267	− 10,640
− 28,451	− 26,861	77,399

623.	624.	625.
65,573	57,268	75,877
29,710	− 40,148	− 43,468
− 18,132	32,138	15,230
− 17,690	− 20,890	− 31,831

626.	627.	628.
77,012	72,300	85,152
− 17,831	− 33,023	− 40,207
− 20,585	46,667	56,242
10,640	− 53,193	− 32,679

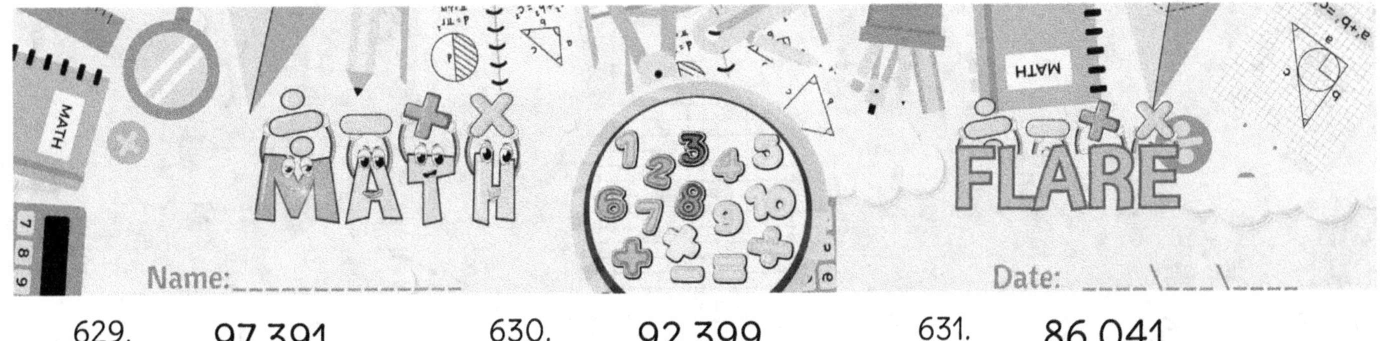

Name: _______________   Date: ____ \ ____ \ ____

629.	630.	631.

629.
```
    97,391
  - 48,150
  - 45,651
    55,746
  _________
```

630.
```
    92,399
  - 41,652
    79,102
  - 29,000
  _________
```

631.
```
    86,041
    45,173
  - 51,293
  - 18,834
  _________
```

632.
```
    58,833
  - 46,305
  - 10,859
    95,620
  _________
```

633.
```
    95,220
    82,893
  - 39,235
  - 34,009
  _________
```

634.
```
    84,645
    78,437
  - 51,438
  - 45,114
  _________
```

635.
```
    72,785
    11,895
  - 54,559
  - 19,973
  _________
```

636.
```
    60,041
  - 14,218
    17,093
  - 35,366
  _________
```

637.
```
    86,734
    70,907
  - 20,298
  - 19,119
  _________
```

638.
```
    89,265
  - 43,196
  - 26,097
    78,452
  _________
```

639.
```
    98,917
  - 38,614
    90,116
  - 14,425
  _________
```

640.
```
    66,536
  - 11,750
    92,972
  - 35,995
  _________
```

641.	642.	643.
62,723	55,971	96,711
51,046	− 54,111	− 15,768
− 12,972	86,066	− 15,087
− 48,706	− 18,172	82,903

644.	645.	646.
87,092	69,039	81,006
− 22,246	− 25,926	− 16,180
37,917	54,200	27,089
− 36,823	− 28,380	− 17,023

647.	648.	649.
71,362	94,160	59,460
90,018	84,026	47,128
− 35,092	− 33,577	− 24,580
− 11,031	− 26,034	− 39,518

650.	651.	652.
56,245	92,419	83,108
− 19,840	− 12,125	67,262
− 24,314	34,815	− 12,133
75,245	− 38,497	− 41,670

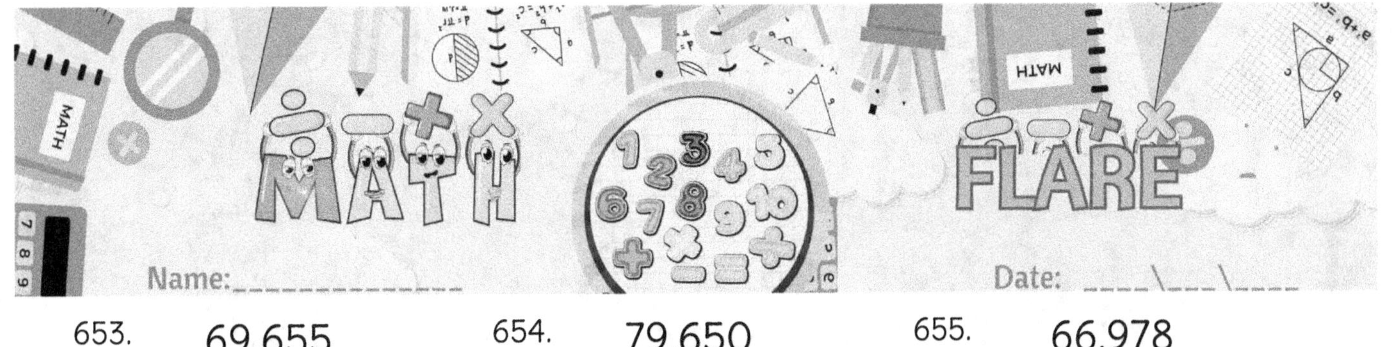

653.	69,655 36,469 - 45,385 - 50,610	654.	79,650 - 33,105 - 46,536 13,086	655.	66,978 - 50,949 - 12,993 21,926
656.	74,018 84,004 - 24,012 - 14,698	657.	82,190 - 44,052 73,980 - 23,528	658.	97,665 - 39,439 61,154 - 14,199
659.	91,532 78,954 - 35,960 - 33,881	660.	93,772 60,094 - 33,914 - 42,732	661.	92,875 86,843 - 41,375 - 35,925
662.	56,626 65,934 - 46,383 - 36,356	663.	73,575 36,075 - 27,539 - 15,296	664.	87,497 - 28,431 - 23,604 10,835

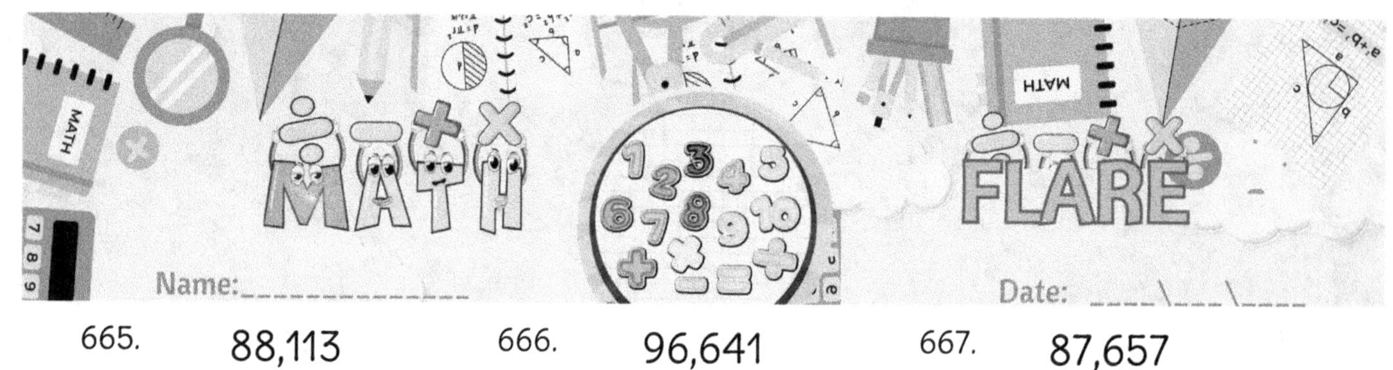

665.	666.	667.
88,113	96,641	87,657
25,418	77,211	- 41,186
- 11,306	- 44,005	18,155
- 49,056	- 40,215	- 45,173

668.	669.	670.
97,145	72,033	60,625
52,213	- 44,610	76,172
- 17,770	36,176	- 13,071
- 41,931	- 35,597	- 54,223

671.	672.	673.
97,668	66,899	75,872
- 15,633	50,560	61,084
89,904	- 26,701	- 45,767
- 39,627	- 28,101	- 41,063

674.	675.	676.
78,740	59,415	78,888
- 39,858	12,319	12,420
- 33,164	- 48,268	- 39,210
18,538	- 14,620	- 49,731

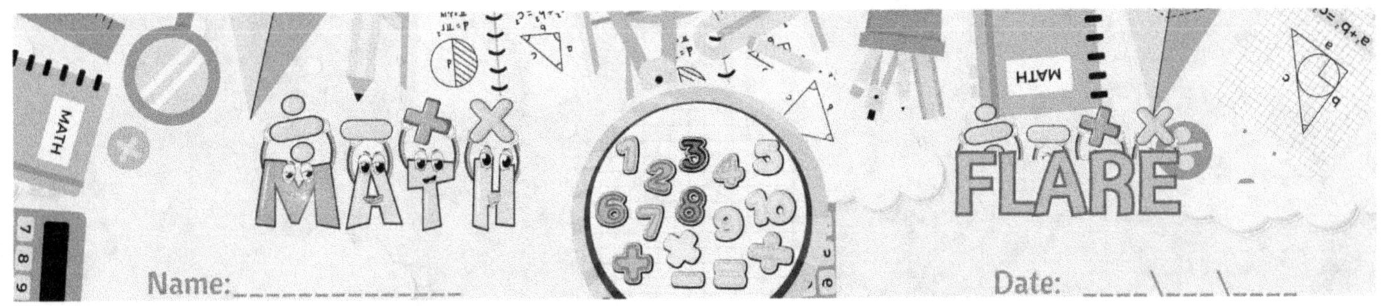

Addition Word Problems

677. Madison has 2 headphones. Her friend gives her 11 more headphones. How many headphones does Madison have now?

678. On Monday, Valentina caught 20 fish, and on Tuesday, Valentina caught 18 fish. How many fish did Valentina catch in total?

679. Luke baked 10 cookies and 9 cupcakes. How many desserts did Luke bake in total?

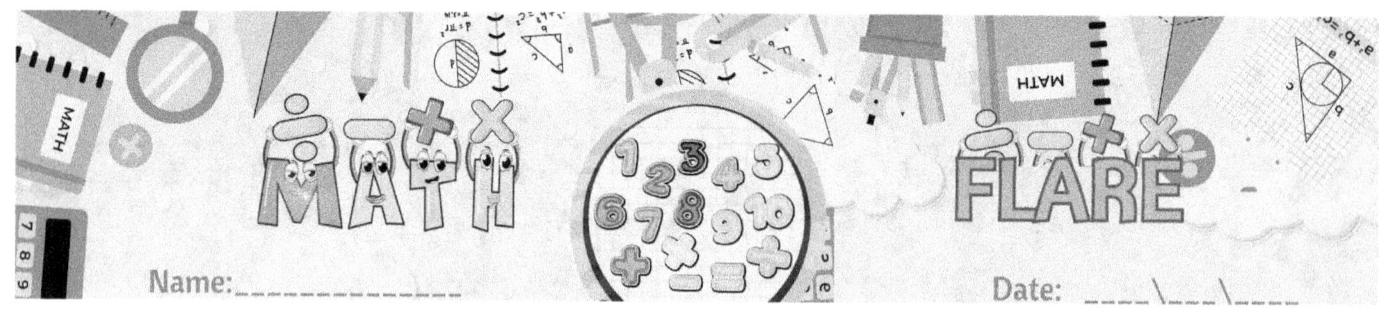

680. Mason has 16 pencils and 13 pens. If Mason puts all the writing utensils in a case, how many writing utensils are in the case in total?

681. Lucas has 7 calculators and buys 20 more calculators. How many calculators does Lucas have in total?

682. Landon played 13 games of chess yesterday and 16 games today. How many games of chess did Landon play in total?

683. Thomas has 19 bandages. He gets 17 more bandages as a gift. How many bandages does Thomas have now?

684. An object has 19 parts. If 12 more parts are added, how many parts does the object have now?

685. A pack of gum contains 20 pieces of gum. If 2 more pieces of gum are added to the pack, how many pieces of gum will the pack contain?

686. At the store, Easton bought 2 coins. Later, Mila bought 5 coins from the same store. How many coins were bought in total?

687. A machine has 18 parts. If 11 more parts are added, how many parts does the machine have now?

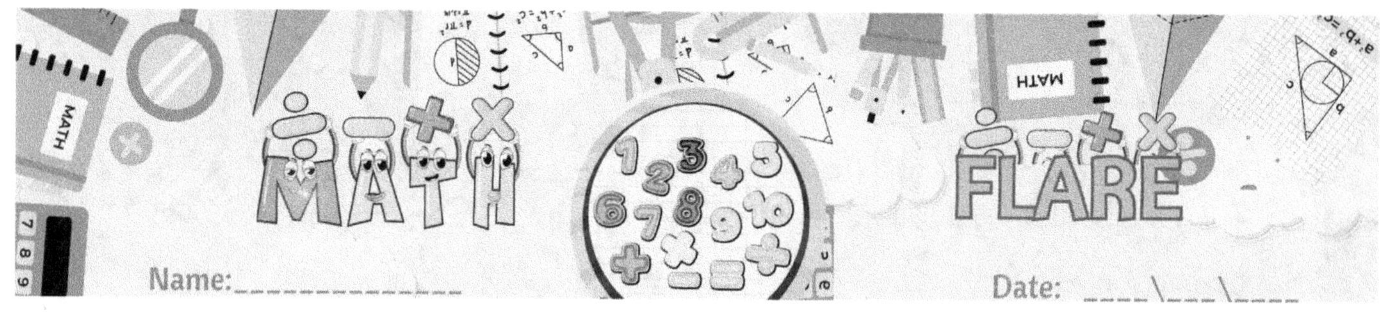

688. A basket holds 14 flosses. If 13 more flosses are added to the basket, how many flosses will the basket hold in total?

689. Maverick drove 11 miles in the morning and 2 miles in the evening. How many miles did Maverick drive in total?

690. Noah has a basket with 4 shirts in it. After buying 3 more shirts, how many shirts does Noah have in total?

691. There are 14 thermometers in the room. 19 more thermometers are brought in. How many thermometers are in the room now?

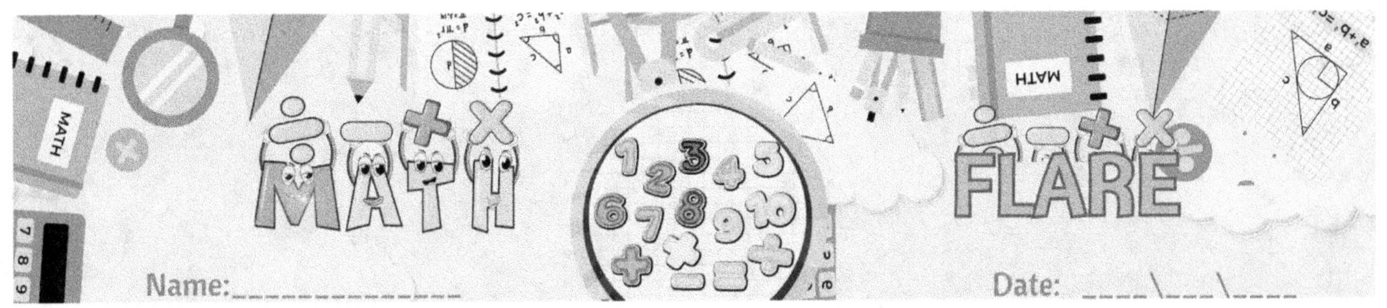

692. Grayson has 9 fish in an aquarium. If Grayson adds 5 more fish to the aquarium, how many fish will be in the aquarium in total?

693. Kingston bought a bag of perfumes for 2 dollars. Later, Kingston bought another bag of perfumes for 18 dollars. How much money did Kingston spend in total?

694. There are 12 trees in the garden. 20 more trees are planted. How many trees are in the garden now?

695. Xavier had 14 dollars and earned 9 more dollars. How much money does Xavier have now?

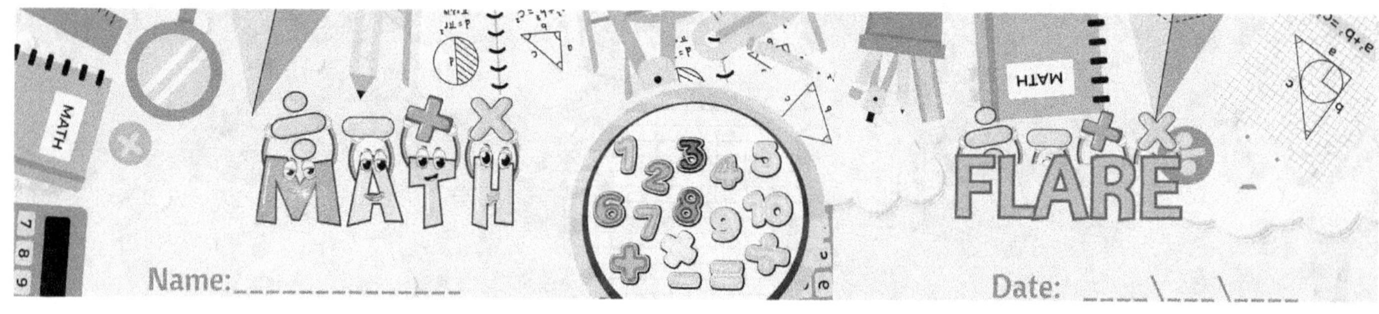

696. Kai has 8 towels and 12 more towels are added to the collection. How many towels does Kai have in total?

697. Aubrey has 14 carrots. She buys 3 more carrots at the store. How many carrots does Aubrey have now?

698. Claire watched 16 movies last week and 9 movies this week. How many movies did Claire watch altogether?

699. Aaliyah planted 20 flowers in the morning and 14 flowers in the afternoon. How many flowers did Aaliyah plant?

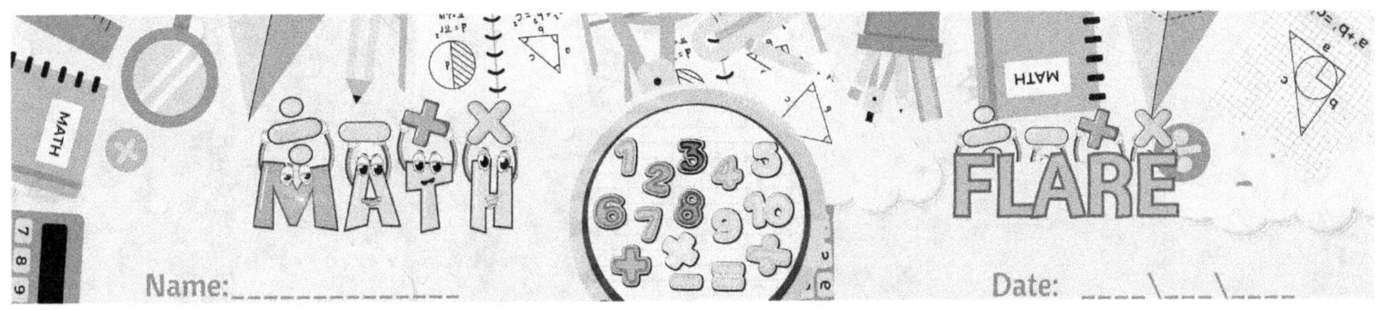

700. Bella sold 19 ointments on Monday and 8 ointments on Tuesday. How many ointments did the she sell in total?

701. There is 1 watch on the shelf. Caroline puts 14 more watches on the shelf. How many watches are there on the shelf now?

702. The weight of an empty container is 12 pounds. If the container is filled with 9 pounds of pencils, what is the total weight of the container and its contents?

703. On Monday, Evelyn read 19 pages, and on Tuesday, 15 pages. How many pages did Evelyn read altogether?

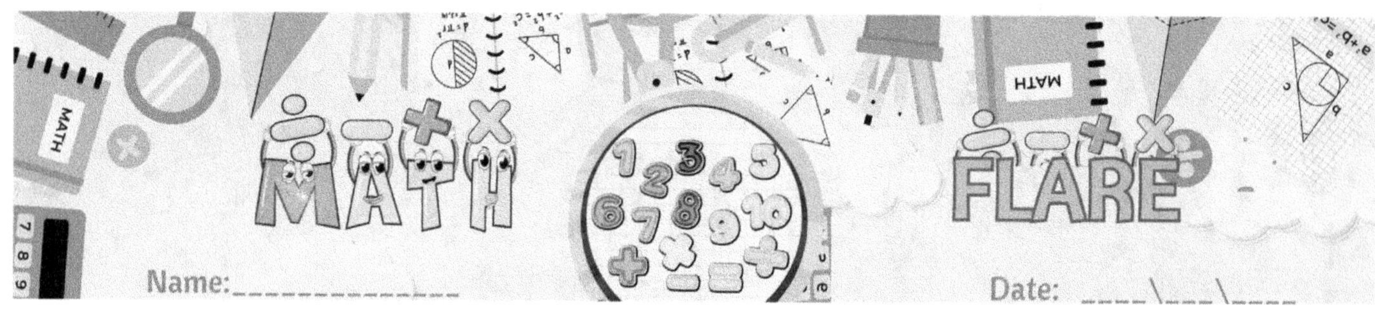

704. A basketball team scored 5 points in the first quarter and 12 points in the second quarter. What was the total score of the basketball team after the first half?

705. Avery has 18 desks. She gets 7 desks from her friend. How many desks does Avery have now?

706. Chase made 8 cookies and Genesis made 8 cookies. How many cookies were made in total?

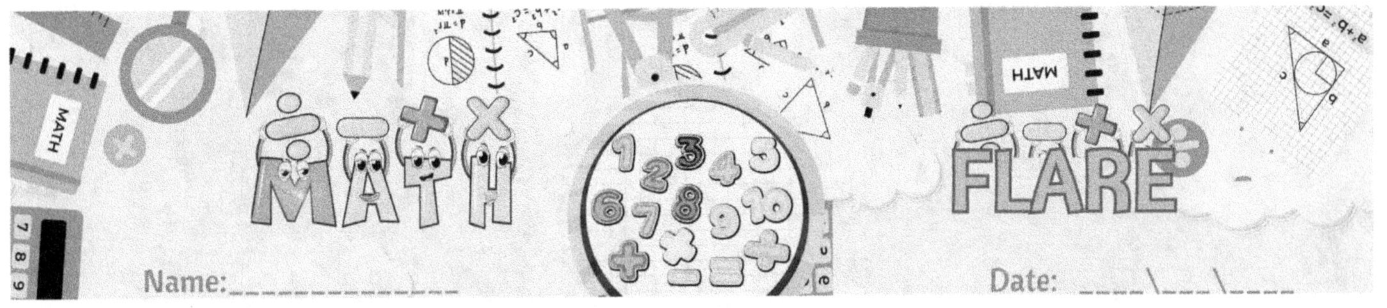

Name:_______________

Date: _______________

Subtraction Word Problems

707. Harper has 5 dollars. She wants to buy combs, which costs 5 dollars. How much more money does she need to buy it?

708. A small bag of chips has 8 chips in it. Landon ate 4 chips. How many chips are left in the bag?

709. Paisley has 14 books. She gave 4 books to Arianna. How many books does Paisley have now?

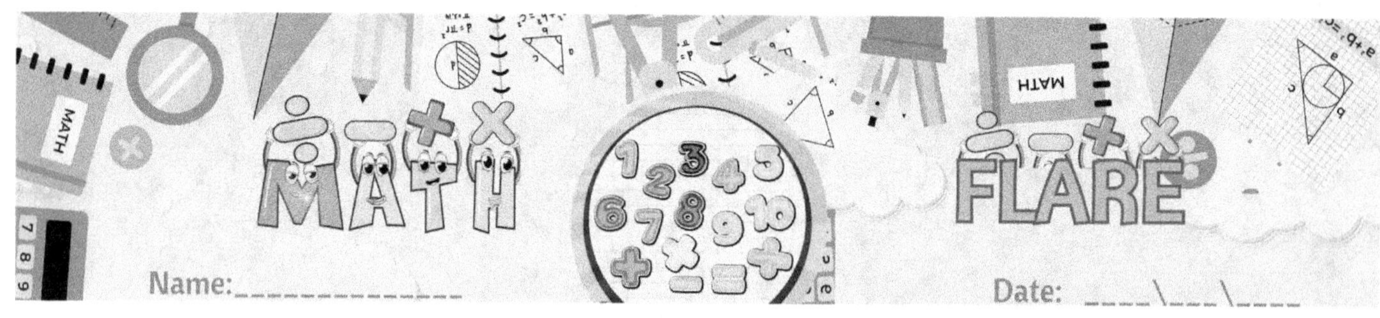

710. Serenity and Peyton went shopping for cotton swabs. They had 20 dollars to spend but 11 dollars ended up being spent. How much money do they have left?

711. A box had 14 chocolates. Luna ate 8 chocolates. How many chocolates are left in the box?

712. Lucas has 16 dollars. He wants to buy toothbrushes that costs 4 dollars. How much more money does he need to buy the toothbrushes?

713. There are 14 turtles in a pond. If 3 leave, how many turtles are left in the pond?

714. A maps costs $16 and a pen costs $16. How much more expensive is the maps than the pen?

715. If you have 8 pencils and you give away 3, how many pencils do you have left?

716. Spoons costs 7 dollars. If you paid $7. How much change will you get back?

717. Brody is 3 years old and Noah is 1 years old. What is the difference in their ages?

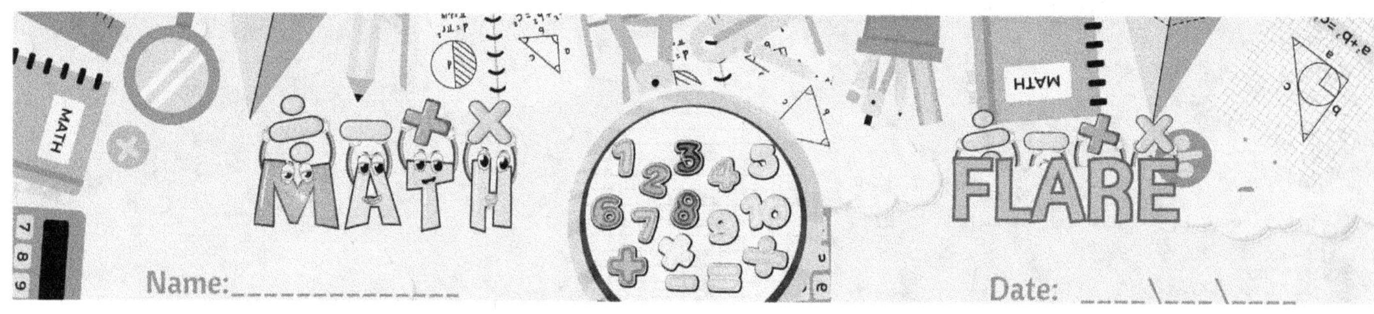

718. If pants costs 20 dollars and you have 1 dollars, how much more money do you need to buy it?

719. Natalie and Trinity went on a shopping spree and bought 3 computers. After returning home, they realized that they didn't need 3 of them. How many computers did they end up keeping?

720. There are 11 watches in a bag. Hailey took 10 watches out of the bag. How many watches are still in the bag?

721. There are 3 fish in a tank. If 3 leave, how many fish are left in the tank?

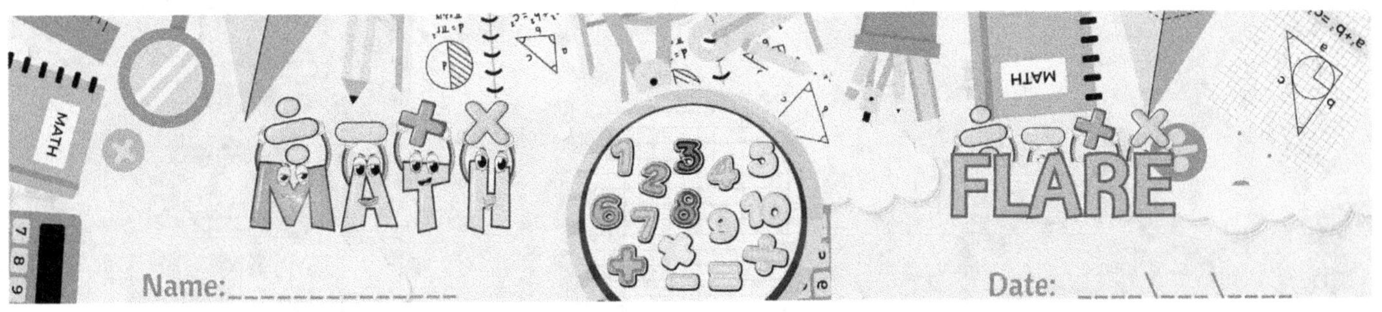

722. There were 1 students in a class. 1 of them were absent. How many students were present in the class?

723. A cake recipe calls for 4 cups of flour. 4 cups of flour have already been added. How many more cups of flour are needed?

724. Toothpastes originally cost 13 dollars, but it is now on sale for 7 dollars. How much money can you save by buying it on sale?

725. Jordan has 4 red bats and 3 green bats. How many more red bats does Jordan have than green bats?

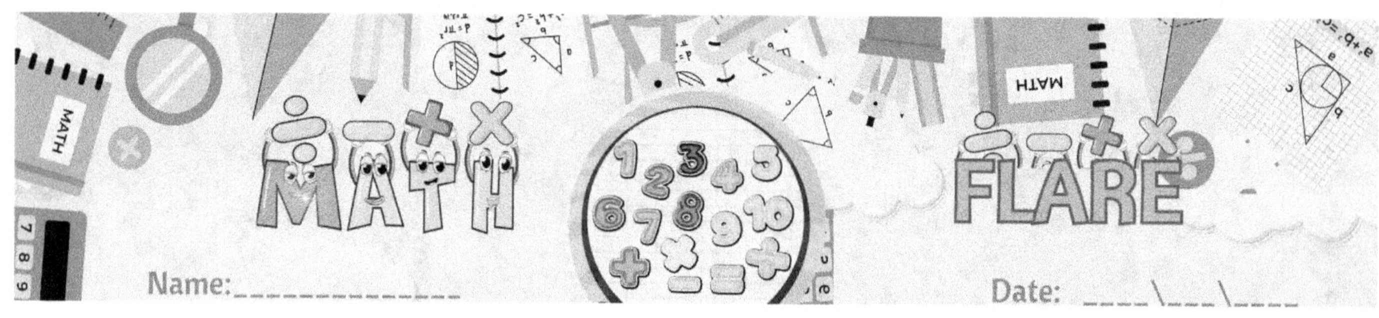

726. Ava wants to buy cups, which costs 20 dollars. She has 12 dollars and plans to save the rest. How much more money does she need to save to buy cups?

727. A recipe needs 3 cups of sugar. Harper added 2 cups of sugar. How many cups of sugar are still needed?

728. There are 6 cars in a parking lot. Oliver took 4 cars out of the lot. How many cars are still in the lot?

729. Bella bought needles for 10 dollars. She received 2 dollars in change. How much did needles cost?

730. There are 11 trees. 5 trees are blue and the rest are red. How many red trees are in the box?

731. Ethan had 7 syringes. He gave 6 syringes to Piper. How many syringes does Ethan have left?

732. A pizza has 7 slices. Olivia ate 1 slices. How many slices of pizza are left?

733. Colton had 4 dollars. He spent 2 dollars on a compasses. How much money does Colton have left?

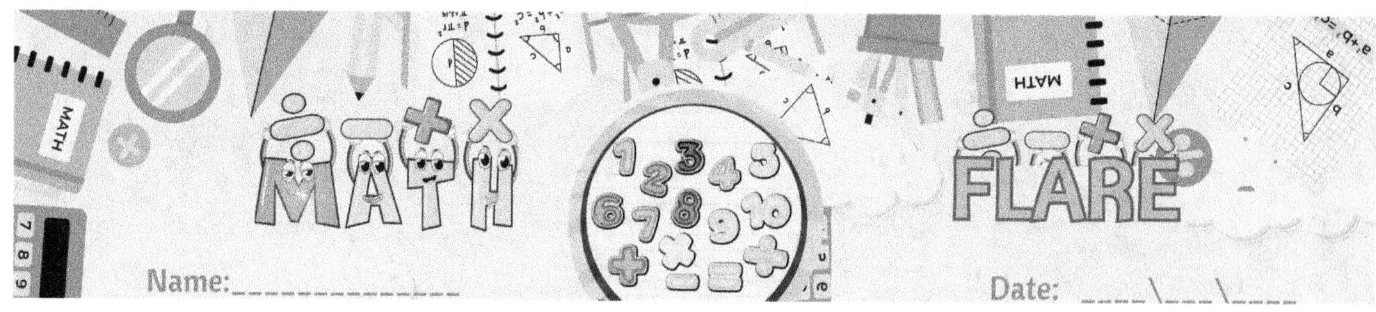

734. Logan has 18 cakes in his collection. He sold 4 of them at a sale. How many cakes does he have left in his collection?

735. Genesis bought clocks for 3 dollars but later found out it was on sale for 3 dollars less. How much did she overpay for clocks?

736. A cake recipe requires 11 cups of sugar. Ellie only has 10 cups of sugar. How many more cups of sugar does Ellie need?

737. Xavier has 10 sticks. He traded 4 of them with his friend. How many sticks does Xavier have now?

ANSWERS

Page 1: Addition with Regrouping

1. 32,131	2. 51,916	3. 82,624	4. 72,432	5. 61,120
6. 103,213	7. 61,140	8. 32,527	9. 21,261	10. 82,122
11. 71,314	12. 21,236	13. 64,340	14. 63,232	15. 37,320
16. 93,630	17. 46,324	18. 81,122	19. 96,411	20. 41,410
21. 21,246	22. 71,411	23. 101,160	24. 73,310	25. 82,510
26. 105,711	27. 51,141	28. 32,183	29. 31,430	30. 71,430
31. 32,312	32. 107,121	33. 43,227	34. 74,420	35. 105,520
36. 83,210	37. 54,110	38. 51,141	39. 81,324	40. 96,211
41. 103,620	42. 71,110	43. 91,130	44. 107,755	45. 66,511
46. 22,560	47. 45,410	48. 41,631	49. 34,315	50. 26,412
51. 51,110	52. 107,310	53. 61,232	54. 61,210	55. 31,411
56. 35,150	57. 82,310	58. 32,342	59. 81,210	60. 101,820
61. 73,620	62. 42,133	63. 95,210	64. 93,124	65. 24,111
66. 41,320	67. 71,311	68. 32,314	69. 73,113	70. 74,461
71. 69,370	72. 85,330	73. 71,210	74. 61,317	75. 105,140
76. 24,242	77. 107,310	78. 81,312	79. 68,686	80. 104,340
81. 102,410	82. 104,610	83. 61,662	84. 91,528	85. 91,110
86. 21,110	87. 51,110	88. 81,362	89. 22,115	90. 71,610

91. 22,321   92. 41,120   93. 68,654   94. 91,381   95. 101,720

96. 73,110   97. 92,124   98. 103,120   99. 21,121   100. 42,434

Page 6: Subtraction with Regrouping

101. 69,489   102. 44,684   103. 62,888   104. 88,787   105. 22,875

106. 58,429   107. 21,469   108. 88,874   109. 4,779   110. 91,879

111. 63,435   112. 30,679   113. 44,872   114. 8,258   115. 89,587

116. 57,849   117. 22,833   118. 56,779   119. 11,873   120. 80,879

121. 11,708   122. 55,885   123. 11,589   124. 60,888   125. 67,859

126. 30,368   127. 24,558   128. 50,859   129. 7,888   130. 53,485

131. 15,347   132. 13,479   133. 37,363   134. 80,789   135. 9,479

136. 34,689   137. 61,789   138. 38,388   139. 50,733   140. 6,177

141. 55,286   142. 91,888   143. 16,469   144. 53,802   145. 92,858

146. 65,685   147. 72,589   148. 26,779   149. 56,869   150. 50,756

151. 59,478   152. 20,477   153. 21,767   154. 82,867   155. 32,549

156. 11,227   157. 28,369   158. 79,845   159. 24,283   160. 67,547

161. 23,489   162. 80,539   163. 46,838   164. 93,785   165. 31,676

166. 25,879   167. 80,864   168. 25,369   169. 66,469   170. 18,482

171. 18,687   172. 18,649   173. 91,649   174. 46,789   175. 61,859

176. 59,788   177. 21,311   178. 17,849   179. 12,687   180. 6,816

181. 56,547   182. 32,829   183. 41,279   184. 73,879   185. 42,277

186. 50,838   187. 61,658   188. 14,585   189. 28,268   190. 12,849

191. 19,688   192. 63,659   193. 82,877   194. 47,679   195. 63,879

196. 65,587

Page 11: Addition Unknown Number

197. 1,121   198. 937   199. 994   200. 547   201. 979

202. 568   203. 1,421   204. 1,230   205. 939   206. 1,565

207. 1,122   208. 796   209. 995   210. 951   211. 188

212. 497   213. 899   214. 471   215. 313   216. 947

217. 684   218. 1,220   219. 1,110   220. 1,222   221. 1,224

222. 898   223. 995   224. 488   225. 796   226. 1,135

227. 889   228. 621   229. 986   230. 1,110   231. 827

232. 797   233. 1,153   234. 1,441   235. 999   236. 1,640

237. 999   238. 1,353   239. 572   240. 1,220   241. 641

242. 1,725   243. 1,110   244. 1,411   245. 997   246. 1,160

247. 994   248. 975   249. 758   250. 1,740   251. 337

252. 417   253. 686   254. 999   255. 881   256. 1,121

257. 893   258. 788   259. 796   260. 596   261. 597

262. 1,640   263. 911   264. 1,360   265. 599   266. 689

267. 1,684   268. 869   269. 1,510   270. 311   271. 1,647

272. 986   273. 789   274. 1,323   275. 1,470   276. 514

277. 1,121   278. 1,410   279. 1,241   280. 939   281. 889

282. 538   283. 1,310   284. 298   285. 882   286. 757

287. 549   288. 416   289. 986   290. 971   291. 1,383

292. 1,310   293. 149   294. 1,717   295. 979   296. 997

297. 674   298. 962

Page 17: Subtraction: Unknown Number

299. 420   300. 975   301. 342   302. 329   303. 277   304. 321

305. 835   306. 199   307. 597   308. 187   309. 94   310. 103

311. 947   312. 102   313. 273   314. 588   315. 144   316. 348

317. 225   318. 159   319. 355   320. 106   321. 5   322. 105

323. 625   324. 199   325. 145   326. 84   327. 185   328. 18

329. 116   330. 861   331. 225   332. 229   333. 455   334. 370

335. 349   336. 248   337. 325   338. 125   339. 124   340. 477

341. 32   342. 184   343. 363   344. 489   345. 255   346. 167

347. 224   348. 123   349. 149   350. 30   351. 27   352. 161

353. 139   354. 156   355. 912   356. 191   357. 744   358. 109

359. 184   360. 811   361. 874   362. 145   363. 127   364. 409

365. 211   366. 174   367. 376   368. 381   369. 449   370. 111

371. 764   372. 293   373. 45   374. 2   375. 130   376. 502

377. 124   378. 190   379. 579   380. 620   381. 33   382. 535

383. 395   384. 269   385. 174   386. 128   387. 145   388. 691

389. 986   390. 299   391. 358   392. 584   393. 353   394. 44

395. 52   396. 951   397. 915   398. 341   399. 655   400. 106

401. 142   402. 113   403. 128   404. 628

Page 23: Addition (3 Addends)

405. 20,104   406. 25,227   407. 21,070   408. 23,762   409. 10,084

410. 19,283   411. 11,114   412. 14,747   413. 21,301   414. 7,006

415. 12,763   416. 15,804   417. 15,716   418. 12,700   419. 11,689

420. 20,609   421. 18,720   422. 23,934   423. 12,983   424. 18,876

425. 24,569   426. 16,623   427. 13,818   428. 11,727   429. 11,944

430. 21,231   431. 16,407   432. 15,269   433. 15,923   434. 10,292

435. 23,509   436. 11,308   437. 15,543   438. 8,308   439. 15,524

440. 16,678   441. 20,450   442. 17,842   443. 16,044   444. 21,835

445. 14,578   446. 22,535   447. 16,626   448. 19,244   449. 13,823

450. 18,035   451. 15,205   452. 20,779   453. 16,632   454. 13,692

455. 17,452   456. 10,149   457. 16,451   458. 19,586   459. 21,491

460. 24,306   461. 21,330   462. 11,489   463. 12,336   464. 19,386

465. 15,355   466. 16,455   467. 16,624   468. 11,635   469. 10,513

470. 13,481   471. 19,008   472. 12,003   473. 8,272   474. 22,911

475. 19,580   476. 12,230   477. 8,981   478. 13,076   479. 18,994

480. 14,800   481. 23,257   482. 19,048   483. 19,895   484. 11,118

485. 18,906   486. 17,438   487. 13,669   488. 14,077   489. 19,218

490. 13,306   491. 12,828   492. 15,060   493. 8,422   494. 21,506

495. 16,539   496. 24,585   497. 24,478   498. 21,906   499. 22,625

500. 12,257   501. 13,935   502. 12,910   503. 20,839   504. 18,906

505. 19,828   506. 20,505   507. 18,399   508. 9,669   509. 13,021

510. 23,290   511. 16,598   512. 14,241   513. 20,531   514. 21,136

515. 13,910   516. 20,116   517. 8,743   518. 17,717   519. 12,682

520. 21,893   521. 16,372   522. 15,588   523. 20,819   524. 14,206

525. 10,064   526. 15,438   527. 10,909   528. 22,370   529. 8,825

530. 16,504   531. 24,976   532. 13,203

Page 31:   Multiple Operations: Addition Subtraction

533. 91,660   534. 94,087   535. 78,278   536. 80,555

537. 127,892   538. 106,071   539. 93,890   540. 76,544

541. 53,751   542. 106,498   543. 54,880   544. 103,026

545. 22,257   546. 69,119   547. 50,450   548. 113,689

549. 135,048   550. 95,277   551. 106,793   552. 31,498

553. 62,738   554. 68,572   555. 8,030   556. 47,141

557. 47,185   558. 53,489   559. 92,087   560. 90,374

561. 104,937   562. 54,098   563. 22,854   564. 85,059

565. 32,360   566. 56,023   567. 95,550   568. 6,357

569. 43,628   570. 17,011   571. 96,637   572. 55,034

573. 45,624   574. 122,221   575. 45,680   576. 97,541

577. 79,791   578. 122,473   579. 103,580   580. 52,206

581. 58,573   582. 76,730   583. 61,289   584. 93,016

585. 68,076   586. 148,261   587. 74,352   588. 50,869

589. 37,767   590. 22,851   591. 57,520   592. 148,545

593. 61,840   594. 47,738   595. 76,267   596. 83,649

597. 82,736   598. 52,009   599. 70,344   600. 93,637

601. 99,873   602. 10,355   603. 50,472   604. 41,615

605. 56,626   606. 73,311   607. 54,440   608. 36,095

609. 51,046   610. 51,853   611. 28,463   612. 82,861

613. 15,618   614. 82,359   615. 29,932   616. 4,408

617. 141,130   618. 46,068   619. 72,966   620. 88,228

621. 126,559   622. 88,711   623. 59,461   624. 28,368

625. 15,808   626. 49,236   627. 32,751   628. 68,508

629. 59,336   630. 100,849   631. 61,087   632. 97,289

633. 104,869   634. 66,530   635. 10,148   636. 27,550

637. 118,224   638. 98,424   639. 135,994   640. 111,763

641. 52,091   642. 69,754   643. 148,759   644. 65,940

645. 68,933   646. 74,892   647. 115,257   648. 118,575

649. 42,490   650. 87,336   651. 76,612   652. 96,567

653. 10,129   654. 13,095   655. 24,962   656. 119,312

657. 88,590   658. 105,181   659. 100,645   660. 77,220

661. 102,418   662. 39,821   663. 66,815   664. 46,297

665. 53,169   666. 89,632   667. 19,453   668. 89,657

669. 28,002   670. 69,503   671. 132,312   672. 62,657

673. 50,126   674. 24,256   675. 8,846   676. 2,367

Page 43: Addition Word Problems

677. 13   678. 38   679. 19   680. 29   681. 27   682. 29   683. 36

684. 31   685. 22   686. 7   687. 29   688. 27   689. 13   690. 7

691. 33   692. 14   693. 20   694. 32   695. 23   696. 20   697. 17

698. 25   699. 34   700. 27   701. 15   702. 21   703. 34   704. 17

705. 25   706. 16

Page 51: Subtraction Word Problems

707. 0   708. 4   709. 10   710. 9   711. 6   712. 12   713. 11

714. 0   715. 5   716. 0   717. 2   718. 19   719. 0   720. 1

721. 0   722. 0   723. 0   724. 6   725. 1   726. 8   727. 1

728. 2   729. 8   730. 6   731. 1   732. 6   733. 2   734. 14

735. 0   736. 1   737. 6